C PROGRAMMING

MIKE McGRATH

In easy steps is an imprint of Computer Step
Southfield Road . Southam
Warwickshire CV47 0FB . United Kingdom
www.ineasysteps.com

Notice of Liability
Every effort has been made to ensure that this book contains accurate and current information. However, Computer Step and the author shall not be liable for any loss or damage suffered by readers as a result of any information contained herein.

Trademarks
All trademarks are acknowledged as belonging to their respective companies.

Printed and bound in the United Kingdom

ISBN 1-84078-203-X

Contents

5 Making statements   53

6 Using functions   65

7 Working with bits   79

Introducing C

Welcome to the exciting world of C programming. This initial chapter introduces the C language with an explanation of its standard "header" libraries and an overview of the C code compilation process. A simple example demonstrates how to create a C program, how to compile it into machine-readable byte code, then how to execute the finished program.

Covers

Chapter One

The C programming language

C is a compact general-purpose programming language that was originally developed by Dennis Ritchie for the Unix operating system. It was first implemented on the Digital Equipment Corporation PDP-11 computer in 1972.

This new programming language was named "C" as it succeeded an earlier programming language named "B" that had been introduced around 1970.

The Unix operating system and virtually all Unix applications are written in the C language. However, C is not limited to a particular platform and programs can be created on any machine that supports C, including those employing the Windows platform.

The flexibility and portability of C made it very popular and the language was formalized in 1988 by the American National Standards Institute (ANSI). The ANSI C standard unambiguously defined each aspect of C, thereby eliminating some uncertainty about the precise syntax of the language.

ANSI C has become the recognized standard for the C language and is described, and demonstrated by examples, in this book.

Why learn C programming?

The C language has been around for quite some time and has seen the introduction of newer programming languages like Java, C++ and C#. Many of these new languages are derived, at least in part, from C, but are much larger in size. The more compact C is better to start out in programming because it is simpler to learn.

It is easier to move on to learn the newer languages once the principles of C programming have been grasped. For instance, C++ is an extension of C and can be difficult to learn unless you have mastered C programming first.

Despite the extra features available in newer languages C remains popular because it is versatile and efficient. It is used today on a large number of platforms for everything from micro-controllers to the most advanced scientific systems. Programmers around the world embrace C because it allows them maximum control and efficiency in their programs.

Standard C libraries

ANSI C defines a number of standard libraries that contain tried and tested functions which can be used in your own C programs. The libraries are known as '"header files" and each have the file extension of ".h". The names of the C standard library header files are listed in the table below with a description of their purpose.

A function is a piece of code that can be reused repeatedly in a C program.
A description of each function in the C library is given in the Appendix to this book, starting on page 161.

Library	Description
stdio.h	Contains input and output functions, types and macro definitions. This library is used by most C programs and represents almost one third of the entire standard C library
ctype.h	Contains functions for testing characters
string.h	Contains functions for manipulating strings
math.h	Contains mathematical functions
stdlib.h	Contains utility functions for number conversion, storage allocation, etc.
assert.h	Contains a function that can be used to add diagnostics to a program
stdarg.h	Contains a function that can be used to step through a list of function arguments
setjmp.h	Contains a function that can be used to avoid the normal call and return sequence
signal.h	Contains functions for handling exceptional conditions that may arise in a program
time.h	Contains functions for manipulating date and time
limits.h	Contains constant definitions for the size of C data types
float.h	Contains constant definitions relating to floating-point arithmetic

The GNU C compiler

C programs are initially created as plain text files, saved with the file extension of ".c". These can be written in any text editor, such as Windows Notepad – no special software is needed.

In order to execute a C program it must first be "compiled" into byte code that can be understood by the computer. A C compiler reads the original text version of the program and translates it into a second file – in a machine-readable executable format.

If the text program contains any syntax errors these will be reported by the compiler and the executable file will not be built.

The complete terms and conditions of the General Public License can be found at http://www.gnu.org/copyleft/gpl.html.

One of the most popular C compilers is the GNU C compiler (GCC) that is available free under the terms of the General Public License (GPL). It is included with virtually every distribution of the Linux operating system. The GNU C compiler is used to compile all the example programs listed in this book into executable byte code.

To discover if you already have the GNU C compiler on your system type **gcc –v** at a command prompt. If available the compiler will respond with version information:

If a C compiler is installed the standard C library header files (listed on the previous page) will also be installed.

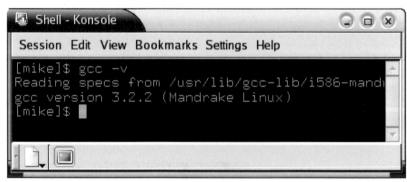

Because C++ is an extension of C, any C++ development tool can also be used to compile C programs.

If you are using the Linux platform and the GNU C compiler is not available on your computer install it from the distribution CD-ROM, or ask your system administrator to install it for you.

If you are using the Windows platform you will need to install the GNU C compiler by following the instructions on the next page.

Installing GCC for Windows

The GNU (pronounced "guh-NEW") Project was launched in 1984 to develop a complete Unix-like operating system as free software. A part of the GNU system is the Minimalist GNU for Windows (MinGW). MinGW includes the GNU C compiler that can be used on Windows systems to create executable C programs.

GNU is a recursive acronym for "GNU's Not Unix".

MinGW download information can be found at
http://www.mingw.org/download.shtml
and the package can be downloaded from
http://sourceforge.net/project/showfiles.php?group_id=2435.

The single-archive MinGW distribution is a tarball named similarly to **MinGW-1.1.tar.gz**.

The excellent free 7-zip compression/ extraction tool can be downloaded from the Web at www.7-zip.com.

After downloading the archive, create a directory on your system that you wish to serve as the base of the installation (**C:\MinGW**). Extract the distribution archive into this directory using a file compression tool like Winzip. If your compression/extraction application does not by default preserve the directory structure of archive contents, be sure that you instruct it to do so manually.

On older versions of Windows add the C:\MinGW\bin address at the end of the Set Path statement in the C:\autoexec.bat file.

The final step is to add the **C:\MinGW\bin** sub-directory of the MinGW installation to your system PATH. In Windows XP open the Environment Variables dialog by clicking the System icon in the Control Panel then select the Advanced tab and push the Environment Variables button. Find the Path variable then edit the end of its statement line to include the address **C:\MinGW\bin**.

To verify that installation completed properly, type **gcc -v** at a command prompt and the GNU C compiler will respond with version information:

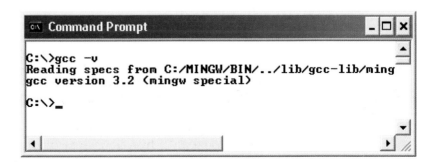

A first C program

In C programs the code statements to be executed are contained inside "functions". Code that defines a function is called a function "declaration" and always has this syntax:

data-type function-name () { statements-to-be-executed }

After a function has been called upon to execute the statements it contains, it returns a value to the caller. This value can only be of the data-type specified in the function declaration.

A program can contain one or many functions but must always have a function called "main". The **main()** function is the starting point of all C programs and the C compiler will not compile the code unless it finds a function called "main" within the program.

Avoid choosing names that begin with an underscore as the C libraries use that naming convention.

Other functions in a program can be given any name you like using letters, digits and the underscore character, but the name may not begin with a digit. Also the C keywords, listed in the Handy Reference on the inner front cover of this book, must be avoided.

The plain brackets that follow the function-name can, optionally, contain values to be used by that function. These take the form of a comma-separated list and are known as function "arguments".

All whitespace is completely ignored by the C compiler.

The curly brackets (braces) contain the statements to be executed whenever the function is called. Each statement must be terminated by a semi-colon, in the same way that English language sentences must be terminated by a full stop.

Traditionally, the first program to attempt when learning any programming language is that which simply generates the message "Hello World". In C, the program code looks like this:

hello.c

```
#include <stdio.h>

int main()
{
  printf("Hello World\n");
  return 0;
}
```

Notice how the code is formatted using spacing (known as whitespace) and indentation to improve its readability.

The program code begins with an instruction to the C compiler to **include** information from the standard input/output library, **stdio.h**. This makes the functions within that library available for use in this program. One of these is a function named **printf()** that is used to write the output from a program.

The instruction is more properly called a "preprocessor" instruction and must be placed at the start of the page, before the actual program code is processed. The **#** hash character starts the line to denote a preprocessor instruction. Notice that the name of the library file must be enclosed by **<** and **>** angled brackets.

In the function declaration the data-type is specified as **int**, meaning integer. This means that after executing its statements this function must return an integer value to the operating system.

As this program contains just one function it must be named as the obligatory **main()** function that is required in all C programs. The plain brackets after the **main()** function-name are empty as no optional arguments have been specified.

Each statement must be terminated with a semi-colon.

The braces contain the statements to be executed by the program. The first statement calls upon the **printf()** function that is defined in the standard input/output library. It specifies as its argument a string of text inside double quotes. In C programming, strings must always be enclosed in double quotes.

This string contains the text "Hello World" and the newline escape sequence **\n**. This is one of the escape sequences listed in the Handy Reference on the inner front cover of this book. It will move the print head to the left margin of the next line following output of the "Hello World" text.

The second and final statement in the **main()** function uses the C keyword **return** to return a value of zero to the operating system. Traditionally returning a zero value after the execution of a program indicates to the operating system that the program executed correctly.

The program in text format is saved with the ".c" file extension as **hello.c** and is ready to be compiled to create an executable version in machine-readable byte code format.

Compiling & running programs

The C source code files for the examples in this book are stored in a directory created expressly for that purpose. The directory is named "MyPrograms" and its absolute address on Windows is **C:\MyPrograms**, whereas on Linux it's at **/home/MyPrograms**.

The **hello.c** program source code file, created on the previous page, is saved in this directory awaiting compilation to produce a version in executable byte code format.

At a command prompt type **gcc --help** *to see a list of all the possible compiler options.*

From a command prompt navigate to the MyPrograms directory, then type **gcc hello.c** to attempt to compile the C program. When the attempt succeeds the compiler creates an executable file alongside the original source code file. By default this file will be called **a.out** on Linux systems and **a.exe** on Windows systems.

Compiling a different C source code file in the MyPrograms directory would now overwrite the first executable file without warning. This is obviously unsatisfactory so a custom name for the executable file must be specified when compiling **hello.c**.

To make the compiler generate an executable file with a specific name use its **-o** option, followed by your preferred file name.

On either Windows or Linux platforms now type the command **gcc hello.c -o hello.exe** at a prompt in the MyPrograms directory. This will compile the **hello.c** source code file and generate an executable file named **hello.exe**.

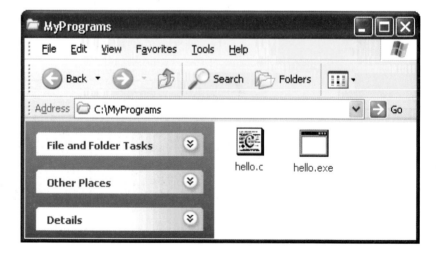

To run the generated executable program file in Windows simply type the file name **hello.exe** at the command prompt in the MyPrograms directory.

*Windows users can even omit the file extension to run programs. In this case, just typing **hello** is sufficient.*

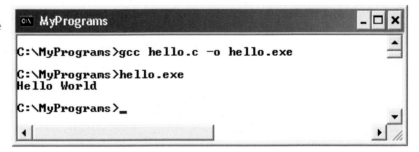

Because Linux does not, by default, look in the current directory for executable files, unless it is specifically directed to do so, it is necessary to prefix the file name with ./ to execute the program.

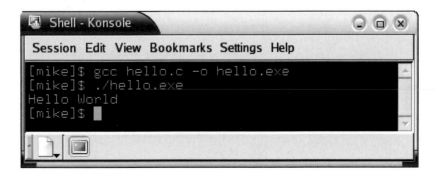

Adding comments

It is good programming practice to add comments to your C source code. This makes the code more easily understood when read by other people, or by yourself when revisiting a piece of code after a period of absence.

Any remarks that appear between /* and */ are ignored by the C compiler, even when spread across multiple lines on the page.

Most commercial C programs begin with a comment block describing the purpose of the program together with other information such as the author's name, date the program was written, copyright permissions, etc..

Comments may also describe the purpose of individual functions and statements. The previous program **hello.c**, listed on page 12, could be enhanced with useful comments like those below:

hello.c
(commented)

```
/*
    This is a first program to introduce C programming.
    Its purpose is to generate the traditional message
    of "Hello World", then move on to a new line.
*/

/*
    First make the standard input/output functions
    in the stdio.h header file available to this program.
*/

#include <stdio.h>

/* declare the obligatory main() function */

int main()
{

  /* call the printf() function to output a string */

  printf("Hello World\n");

  /* return zero to confirm that the program ran OK */

  return 0;
}
```

This is ideally how C source code should be commented – the examples in this book are largely uncommented, however, because of space limitations.

Storing data

This chapter introduces the basic "variable" object that is used to store data for manipulation in a C program. It is called a variable because the data that it contains can be varied as the program proceeds. Examples demonstrate how to create variables which can store different types of data and how the stored data can be used in a program.

Covers

Chapter Two

Creating variables

A variable is like a container in a C program in which a data value can be stored inside the computer's memory. The stored value can be referenced using the variable's name. The programmer can choose any name for a variable providing it follows the naming conventions listed in the table below:

Variable names are case-sensitive in C – so variables named "VAR", "Var" and "var" would be treated as three separate variables by the program.

Naming rule	Example	Accept
Cannot start with a number	2bad	X
Can contain a number elsewhere	good1	✓
Cannot contain arithmetical operators	a+b*c	X
Cannot contain punctuation characters	%£#@!!	X
Can contain the underscore character	_is_good	✓
Cannot contain any spaces	no spaces	X
Can be of mixed cases	UPdown	✓
Cannot contain any of the C keywords	volatile	X

C keywords are listed in a table on the inner front cover of this book.

It is good practice to choose meaningful names for variables to make the program more easily understood.

To create a variable in a program requires it to be "declared". A variable declaration has this syntax:

data-type variable-name ;

First the declaration specifies which type of data the variable is permitted to contain. This will be one of the four data types described on the opposite page. The type is followed by a space then the chosen variable name, adhering to the naming rules. Finally the declaration is terminated by a semi-colon. This is used much like a full stop in the English language to mark the end of a sentence. Multiple variables of the same data type can be created in a single declaration by separating the variable names with a comma:

data-type variable1, variable2, variable3 ;

There are four basic data types in the C language. These are defined using the C keywords which are listed in the following table, together with a description of each data type:

Data type	Description	Example
char	a single byte, capable of holding one character	A
int	an integer whole number	100
float	a floating-point number, correct up to six decimal places	0.123456
double	a floating-point number, correct up to ten decimal places	0.0123456789

The four data types allocate different amounts of machine memory for storing data. The smallest is the **char** data type, which allocates just a single byte of memory, and the largest is the double data type. The **double** data type allocates twice the amount of memory that the **float** data type does, so it should only be used when a precise lengthy floating point number is absolutely required.

Variable declarations should be made before any executable code appears in a program. When a value is assigned to a variable that variable is said to have been "initialized". Optionally a variable may be initialized when it is declared.

The example code fragment below creates a variety of variables and initializes them with appropriate values:

Values of the **char** *data type must always be enclosed by single quotes – double quotes are incorrect.*

```
int num1, num2;          /* declare 2 int variables */
char letter;             /* declare a char variable */
float decimal = 7.5;     /* declare and initialize a
                                        float variable */

num1 = 100;         /* initialize the int variables */
num2 = 200;

letter = 'A';       /* initialize the char variable */
```

Displaying variable values

The value of variables can be displayed using the **printf()** function that was used in chapter 1 to display the "Hello World" message. The desired format in which to display the variable value must be specified as an argument in the **printf()** function's parentheses using a "format specifier", along with the variable name. The table below describes format specifiers that can be used for this purpose:

*Single **char** characters must be enclosed by <u>single</u> quotes – a string of characters, on the other hand, must be enclosed by <u>double</u> quotes.*

Format specifier	Description	Example
%d	an integer whole number	100
%f	a floating point number	0.123456
%c	a single character	'A'
%s	a string of characters	"Hello World"
%p	a machine memory address	0x0022FF5C

The example program code below demonstrates the declaration of a variable of the **double** data type. It is initialized, with an appropriate value, then its value is displayed in the program output.

firstvar.c

```
#include <stdio.h>

int main()
{
    double pi = 3.1415926536;
    printf("The value of pi is approximately %f", pi );
    return 0;
}
```

*Notice how, in this example, the **double** value is rounded up to fit the default **%f** format size of just six decimal places. The format specifier can also specify the precision of the output – in this case **%.10f** would display all the decimal places in the pi variable*

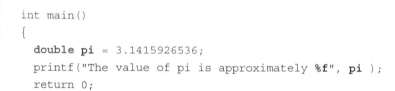

```
C:\MyPrograms>gcc firstvar.c -o firstvar.exe

C:\MyPrograms>firstvar
The value of pi is approximately 3.141593
C:\MyPrograms>_
```

Inputting variable values

Strings are a special case and are demonstrated with the topic of arrays, on page 30.

The "scanf()" function can be used to get input into a program and it requires two arguments. First a format specifier defines the type of data to be entered, then the name of the a variable in which the input will be stored. The variable name must be preceded by a "&" character, except when the data being entered is a string of text. The **&** character, in this case, is the "addressof" operator that directs the input to be stored in the variable name that it precedes.

The **scanf()** function can set the value of multiple variables simultaneously too. The first argument must then contain a list of required format specifiers, each separated by a space, and the entire list should be enclosed by double quotes. The second argument must contain a comma-separated list of variable names to which each specified format applies.

In the following example, the program requests data to be entered which is then assigned to three variables by the **scanf()** function.

setvars.c

```
#include <stdio.h>

int main()
{
    char character; int a,b;
    printf("Enter any one keyboard character: ");
    scanf( "%c", &character );
    printf("Enter 2 integers separated by a space: ");
    scanf( "%d %d", &a, &b );
    printf("The letter entered was %c\n", character);
    printf("Integers entered were %d and %d\n", a, b);
    return 0;
}
```

Note that the **scanf()** *function stops reading input when it encounters a blank space.*

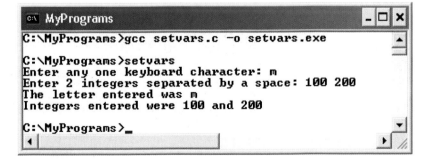

Formatting output

The format specifiers listed in the table on page 20 can be used to control how output appears. A program can ensure that output occupies a specific minimum number of spaces by specifying the required number in the format specifier. The number must be placed immediately after the **%** character in the format specifier. For instance, to ensure that an integer always fills at least 7 spaces the format specifier is **%7d**.

If it is preferable for the blank spaces to be filled with zeros just add a zero between the **%** character and the specified number. To ensure that an integer always fills at least 7 spaces, and that any blank spaces are filled with zeros, the format specifier is **%07d**.

formatspaces.c

This example adds blank and zero-filled spaces to the output – only if the number stated in the format specifier is greater than the number of spaces occupied by the integer.

```c
#include <stdio.h>
int main()
{
    int num = 1;
    printf("Using %%0d  displays %0d\n", num);
    printf("Using %%1d  displays %1d\n", num);
    printf("Using %%2d  displays %2d\n", num);
    printf("Using %%3d  displays %3d\n", num);
    printf("Using %%4d  displays %4d\n", num);
    printf("Using %%05d displays %05d\n", num);
    printf("Using %%06d displays %06d\n", num);
    printf("Using %%07d displays %07d\n", num);
    return 0;
}
```

To display a "%" character with the printf() function prefix it with another "%" character – as seen here.

```
MyPrograms                                        _ □ ✕

C:\MyPrograms>gcc formatspaces.c -o formatspaces.ex

C:\MyPrograms>formatspaces
Using %0d  displays 1
Using %1d  displays 1
Using %2d  displays  1
Using %3d  displays   1
Using %4d  displays    1
Using %05d displays 00001
Using %06d displays 000001
Using %07d displays 0000001

C:\MyPrograms>_
```

Greater control over the output appearance of floating-point numbers can be gained by adding a "precision specifier" to the **%f** format specifier. This is simply a full stop followed by a number representing the desired number of decimal places to be displayed. For instance, a format specifier of **%.2f** will display a floating-point number showing just 2 decimal places.

The minimum space specifier, described on the opposite page, can be combined with the precision specifier so that both number of minimum spaces and number of decimal places can be controlled. For instance, a format specifier of **%07.2f** would display seven spaces, with two decimal places, and any empty spaces would be filled with zeros.

By default, any empty spaces precede the number so it is right-aligned. To have the number displayed left-aligned, with any empty spaces added after the number, prefix the minimum space specifier with a minus sign, as in the example below. The "end" strings are just there to show that empty spaces have been added.

precision.c

```c
#include <stdio.h>
int main()
{
   float num = 7.123456;
   printf("%-8.0f end\n", num);
   printf("%-8.2f end\n", num);
   printf("%-8.4f end\n", num);
   printf("%-8.6f end\n", num);
   return 0;
}
```

The decimal places may be rounded – in this example the number to 4 decimal places has been rounded up to 7.1235.

```
MyPrograms                                    _ □ ✕
C:\MyPrograms>gcc precision.c -o precision.exe

C:\MyPrograms>precision
7        end
7.12     end
7.1235   end
7.123456 end

C:\MyPrograms>_
```

Data type qualifiers

When an **int** variable is declared it can by default contain either positive of negative integer values. These are known as "signed" values. The range of possible values is determined by your system.

If the **int** variable is created by default as a "long" type it typically will have a possible range of values from a maximum of +2147483647 down to a minimum of -2147483648.

On the other hand, if the **int** variable is created by default as a "short" type then typically the maximum possible value will be +32767 and its minimum will be -32768.

The size can be specified when declaring the variable using the **short** and **long** keywords, as demonstrated in this code fragment:

```
short int num1;      /* saves memory space */

long int num2;       /* allows bigger range */
```

Constant values are always referred to in uppercase to distinguish them from variable values.

The **limits.h** header file contains implementation-defined limits for the size of each data type. These are accessed via "constant" values called **INT_MAX** and **INT_MIN**, for **int** variable declarations that do not specify a size. Similarly, **SHRT_MAX** and **SHRT_MIN** for **short int** variable declarations and **LONG_MAX** and **LONG_MIN** for **long int** variable declarations.

The code below displays each of these ranges, shown in the illustration at the top of the opposite page:

maxmin.c

*The code must first **include** the **limits.h** header file in order to have access to its features.*

```
#include <stdio.h>
#include <limits.h>

int main()
{
    printf("Max int: %d\t", INT_MAX );
    printf("Min int: %d\n", INT_MIN );
    printf("Max short: %d\t", SHRT_MAX );
    printf("Min short: %d\n", SHRT_MIN );
    printf("Max long: %d\t", LONG_MAX );
    printf("Min long: %d\n", LONG_MIN );
    return 0;
}
```

A non-negative "unsigned" **int** can be declared with the **unsigned** keyword. An **unsigned short int** variable will typically have a possible range from 0 to 65,535. An **unsigned long int** variable will typically have a possible range from 0 to 4,294,967,295.

The **sizeof** operator is used in this example to examine the amount of memory space allocated to various data types:

sizeof.c

```c
#include <stdio.h>
int main()
{
  printf("short int: %d bytes\t",sizeof(short int));
  printf("long int: %d bytes\n", sizeof(long int));
  printf("unsigned long int: %d bytes\n",
                          sizeof(unsigned long int));
  printf("char: %d byte\t",sizeof(char));
  printf("float: %d bytes\t",sizeof(float));
  printf("double: %d bytes\t\n", sizeof(double));
  return 0;
}
```

Notice how the \t escape sequence is used to format the output.

The default size of memory space allocated to a variable is system-dependent.

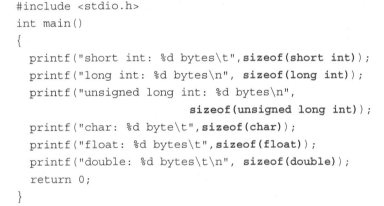

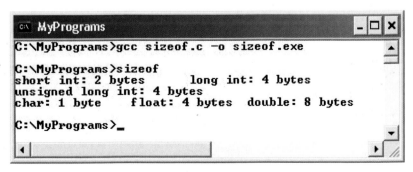

External variables

The extent to which a variable is accessible in a program is called the "variable scope". Variables declared internally inside a function are known as "local" variables, whereas variables that are declared externally outside of a function are known as "global" variables.

Local variables can only be accessed by the function in which they are declared. They come into existence when the function is called and normally disappear when the function is exited.

Global variables, on the other hand, can be accessed by all functions in a program. They remain in existence permanently so are useful to communicate data between functions.

The true value of external variables is more apparent in programs that have multiple functions.

An external global variable must be defined exactly once at the start of the program. It must also be declared at the start of each function that wants to use it. Each declaration should begin with the **extern** keyword which denotes that it is for a global variable, rather than for a regular local variable. These declarations should not be used to initialize the global variable.

The example below demonstrates how to define , declare and initialize an external global variable called "num":

extvars.c

```
#include <stdio.h>

int num;                  /* define an external variable */

int main()
{
   extern int num;    /* declare the external variable */
   num=5;             /* initialize the external variable */
   printf("Global variable value is %d", num);
   return 0;
}
```

```
MyPrograms                                    _ □ ✕

C:\MyPrograms>gcc extvars.c -o extvars.exe

C:\MyPrograms>extvars
Global variable value is 5
C:\MyPrograms>_
```

Static variables

Larger C programs consist of multiple source code files that are compiled together to create a final executable file. This is a very useful aspect of C programming that allows source code to be modular so that it can be reused in different programs.

Global external variables, as described on the opposite page, would normally be accessible to any function in any of the files being compiled together. All functions are normally accessible globally too. Functions and, more usually, external variables can have their accessibility limited to just the file in which they are created by the use of the **static** keyword.

Internal variables can also be declared as static – these are only accessible by the function in which they are declared but they do not disappear when the function is exited. This offers permanent private storage within a function.

Normally a program cannot employ more than one variable of any given name. Using **static** external variables, however, usefully allows external variables of the same name to coexist happily providing they are declared as **static** and are not in the same file. Programming with multiple source code files can find a common external variable name duplicated in two files. Declaring these as **static** avoids the need to rename one of these variables in each occurrence within the source code.

The example below creates a static global external variable that cannot be used by other source code files. Attempting to do so causes an error at compile-time and the compilation will halt.

static.c

```
#include <stdio.h>
static int num=100;/* define static external variable */

int main()
{
    extern int num;      /* declare the external variable */
    printf("Global value: %d", num);
}
```

```
C:\MyPrograms>gcc static.c -o static.exe

C:\MyPrograms>static
Global value: 100
C:\MyPrograms>_
```

Register variables

A **register** variable declaration informs the compiler that the specified variable will be heavily-used by the program. The intention is for the compiler to place **register** variables in the machine registers of the computer to speed access times. Their usefulness may be questionable though as compilers are free to ignore this advice.

A variable declared with the "volatile" keyword is not allowed to be stored in a machine register – this is the opposite effect to a *register* variable.

Only local internal variables can be declared as **register** variables. In any case only a few variables can be kept in registers and they may only be of certain types. The precise limitations vary from machine to machine.

Despite these possible drawbacks **register** declarations are harmless because the **register** keyword is ignored when the compiler cannot actually use machine registers to store the variable. Instead, the variable is created as though the **register** keyword was not there.

One of the principle sorts of variable that might benefit from being a **register** variable is that used to store the control value of a loop. On each iteration of the loop that variable value must be compared and changed so the variable is being repeatedly accessed. Loops are covered in chapter 5, but the loop example below is included here to illustrate the repeated access of an intended **register** variable.

register.c

```
#include <stdio.h>
int main()
{
  register int num=0;

  while( num < 5)
  { ++num; printf(" Pass %d |", num); }
  return 0;
}
```

The loop code in this example instructs that while the value stored in the variable called "num" is below 5 it should add 1 to that value and output a text string that includes its current value on each iteration of the loop.

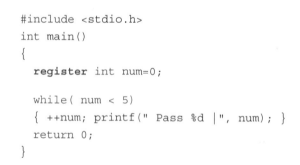

```
C:\MyPrograms>gcc register.c -o register.exe

C:\MyPrograms>register
 Pass 1 | Pass 2 | Pass 3 | Pass 4 | Pass 5 |
C:\MyPrograms>_
```

Converting data types

Any data stored in a variable can be forced (coerced) into a variable of a different data type by a process known as "casting". A cast just states the data type to which the value should be converted in plain brackets before its variable name, like this:

variable-name = (*data-type*) *variable-name* ;

The example below casts both **float** and **char** values into **int** type variables:

cast.c

```c
#include <stdio.h>
int main()
{
    int num1, num2;             /* declare int variables */
    float dec;                  /* declare a float variable */
    char letter;                /* declare a char variable */

    dec = 7.5;          /* initialize the float variable */
    letter = 'A';       /* initialize the char variable */

    num1 = (int) dec;           /* cast float into an int */
    num2 = (int) letter;        /* cast char into an int */

    printf("num1 is: %d\n",num1);
    printf("num2 is: %d\n",num2);
    return 0;
}
```

*Note that the **float** value in this example is simply truncated when cast into the **int** variable – it is not rounded.*

"ASCII" (pronounced "as-kee") stands for "American Standard Code for Information Interchange" and is the accepted standard for plain text. You can see the full range of standard ASCII codes on pages 162 and 163.

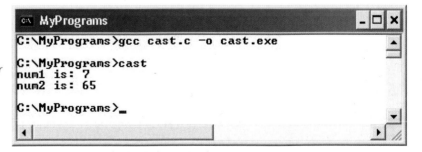

Characters are represented by a numerical ASCII code within the range of 0 - 127. The uppercase letter 'A' in this example is represented by the ASCII numerical code of 65, so that is its integer value when cast into an **int** type variable.

Arrays

An array is a variable that can store multiple items of data, unlike a regular variable which can only store a single item of data.

The pieces of data are stored sequentially in array "elements" that are numbered, starting at zero. So the first array value is stored in array element zero, the second array value is stored in array element 1, and so on.

An array is declared in a C program in the same way as regular variables but additionally the size of the array should be specified in the declaration. This should be stated in square brackets following the array name, with this syntax:

data-type array-name [number-of-elements] ;

Array elements start numbering at zero, not one.

Optionally, an array can be initialized when it is declared by assigning values to each element as a comma-separated list enclosed by curly brackets (braces).

Individual elements can be referenced using the array name followed by square brackets containing the element number.

This example creates an array of three elements and assigns initial values to them. The second element is then changed before each value is displayed in the program output.

array.c

It is acceptable to omit the number from the square brackets (to create an unsized array) if the elements are being initialized in the array declaration – the size will be adjusted automatically to fit the number of elements assigned to that array.

```c
#include <stdio.h>

int main()
{
  /* create an integer array with three elements */
  int arr[3] = { 10,2,8 };

  /* change the value of the array's second element */
  arr[1] = 9;

  /* display the value stored inside each element */
  printf("element 0 contains %d\n", arr[0] );
  printf("element 1 contains %d\n", arr[1] );
  printf("element 2 contains %d\n", arr[2] );

  return 0;
}
```

```
MyPrograms                                            _ □ ✕
C:\MyPrograms>gcc array.c -o array.exe

C:\MyPrograms>array
element 0 contains 10
element 1 contains 9
element 2 contains 8

C:\MyPrograms>_
```

When creating an array to hold a string remember to allow space for an element at the end to contain the null character.

One of the most significant uses of arrays in C programming concerns their ability to store strings of text. Each element in an array of the **char** data type can store a single character. Adding the special **\0** null character escape sequence in the array's final element promotes the array to string status.

An entire string can be referenced using just the array name and can be displayed using the **%s** format specifier.

The example below creates an array with five elements – to contain a four-letter string plus the **\0** null character string terminator. This entire string is then displayed by the program's output.

string.c

```c
#include <stdio.h>
int main()
{
    char arr[5] = { 'm','i','k','e','\0' };

    printf("The array contains the string %s\n", arr );

    return 0;
}
```

```
MyPrograms                                            _ □ ✕
C:\MyPrograms>gcc string.c -o string.exe

C:\MyPrograms>string
The array contains the string mike

C:\MyPrograms>_
```

Multi-dimensional arrays

An array can have more than one index – to represent multiple dimensions, rather than the single dimension of a regular array.

Multi-dimensional arrays of three indices and more are uncommon, but 2-dimensional arrays are useful to store grid-based information such as coordinates.

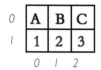

The following example creates a 2-dimensional array with each index having three elements. This represents a table of two rows and three columns. The first row, or index, contains characters and the second row, or index, contains numbers.

Notice the arrangement of the braces to assign initial values to each element of the indices in the array declaration.

array2d.c

Note that the assigned characters in this example are stored as their ASCII integer value then converted back to characters for display by the **%c** format specifier.

```c
#include <stdio.h>
int main()
{
  int arr[3][3] = { {'A','B','C'} , { 1,2,3 }  };

  printf("array [0][0] contains %c\n", arr[0][0] );
  printf("array [0][1] contains %c\n", arr[0][1] );
  printf("array [0][2] contains %c\n", arr[0][2] );

  printf("array [1][0] contains %d\n", arr[1][0] );
  printf("array [1][1] contains %d\n", arr[1][1] );
  printf("array [1][2] contains %d\n", arr[1][2] );

  return 0;
}
```

```
MyPrograms                                    _ □ ✕

C:\MyPrograms>gcc array2d.c -o array2d.exe

C:\MyPrograms>array2d
array [0][0] contains A
array [0][1] contains B
array [0][2] contains C
array [1][0] contains 1
array [1][1] contains 2
array [1][2] contains 3

C:\MyPrograms>_
```

Setting constant values

Constants provide another way to store data in a C program. Unlike variables the initial value assigned to a constant may not be changed during the course of a program. This chapter demonstrates different ways that fixed constants can be created.

Covers

Chapter Three

Declaring constants

A constant can be declared in the same way as a variable but preceded by the **const** keyword. It should be initialized by assigning its permanent value in the declaration. The program may not subsequently assign a different value to the constant.

The example program below calculates the area and circumference of a circle from a diameter value supplied by the user. Both calculations use Pi. The value of Pi will not change so can usefully be assigned to a constant. Notice that it is convention to use uppercase characters for constant names, to readily distinguish them from variable names in the program code.

const.c

```
#include <stdio.h>
int main()
{
   const float PI = 3.141593;
   int diameter;
   float radius, circ, area;

   printf("\nEnter the diameter of a ");
   printf(" circle in millimeters: ");
   scanf("%d", &diameter);

   circ =   (float) PI * diameter;
   radius = (float) diameter / 2;
   area =   (float) PI * (radius * radius);

   printf("\tIts circumference is %.2f mm\n", circ);
   printf("\tAnd its area is %.2f sq.mm\n ", area);
   return 0;
}
```

*The * asterisk character in this code is the arithmetical multiplication operator, and the / forward slash character is the arithmetical division operator. Operators are demonstrated fully in the next chapter.*

The result of each calculation in this example is forced to be a float data type by casting – see page 29.

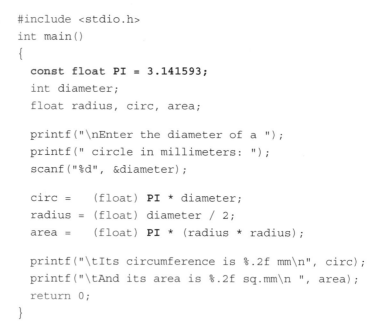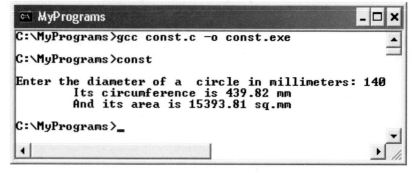

```
C:\MyPrograms>gcc const.c -o const.exe

C:\MyPrograms>const

Enter the diameter of a  circle in millimeters: 140
        Its circumference is 439.82 mm
        And its area is 15393.81 sq.mm

C:\MyPrograms>_
```

Enumerating constants

The **enum** keyword provides a handy way to create a sequence of integer constants in a concise manner. Optionally the declaration can include a name for the sequence after the **enum** keyword. The constant names follow as a comma-separated list within braces.

Each of the constants will by default have a value 1 greater than the constant that it follows in the list. Unless specified the first constant will have a value of zero, the next a value of 1, and so on.

The constants can be assigned any individual value but the following constants will always increment it one by one.

This example represents the points value of balls in the game of snooker starting at 1 for the red ball, right up to 7 for the black ball. The sequence is named "colors" but this could have been omitted.

enum.c

Assigning a value of 1 to the BLUE constant in this example would automatically make the PINK constant 2 and the BLACK constant 3.

```c
#include <stdio.h>
int main()
{
    enum colors
        {RED=1,YELLOW,GREEN,BROWN,BLUE,PINK,BLACK};
    int total;

    printf("I potted a red worth %d\n", RED );
    printf("Then a black worth %d\n", BLACK );
    printf("Followed by another red worth %d\n", RED );
    total = RED + BLACK + RED;
    printf("Altogether I scored %d\n",total);
    return 0;
}
```

```
MyPrograms                                    _ □ ×

C:\MyPrograms>gcc enum.c -o enum.exe

C:\MyPrograms>enum
I potted a red worth 1
Then a black worth 7
Followed by another red worth 1
Altogether I scored 9

C:\MyPrograms>_
```

Creating a constant type

Once an enumerated sequence has been declared it can be considered as a new data type in its own right with properties of its specified constant names, and their associated values.

Variables of this data type can be declared like any other variable using the syntax:

data-type variable-name ;

The example below builds on the previous example which created a data-type called **colors**. A new variable of that type is declared with the name of "fingers". This variable can be assigned any of the constant names specified in the **colors** enumeration list. In this case it is assigned the sum of the **PINK** (6) and **BROWN** (4) constant values:

enumtypes.c

The addition of *PINK* and *BROWN* values (6+4) returns an *int* data type (10). So the cast is essential to assign this value to the *fingers* variable – which is an *enum colors* data type, not *an int* type.

```c
#include <stdio.h>
int main()
{
    /* declare a sequence of constants */
    enum colors
    { RED=1,YELLOW,GREEN,BROWN,BLUE,PINK,BLACK };

    /* declare a variable of the enumerated data type */
    enum colors fingers;

    /* assign valid constants from the colors list */
    fingers = (enum colors) PINK + BROWN;

    /* display the value in the variable */
    printf("value: %d\n", fingers);

    return 0;
}
```

```
C:\ MyPrograms                                    _ □ ×
C:\MyPrograms>gcc enumtypes.c -o enumtypes.exe

C:\MyPrograms>enumtypes
value: 10

C:\MyPrograms>_
```

Custom data types can be defined using the **typedef** keyword. A custom type declaration has this syntax:

typedef *definition* *type-name* ;

The creation of two custom data types is illustrated in the following example. The first is a data type called **COLORS** of the **enum colors** type from the previous example. The second is a data type called **USHRT** of the **unsigned short int** type. Declaring custom data types can make program code more concise.

typedef.c

```
#include <stdio.h>

/* declare a sequence of constants */
enum colors { RED=1,YELLOW,GREEN,BROWN,BLUE,PINK,BLACK};

/* declare a custom type, of the enum colors type */
typedef enum colors COLORS;

/* declare a custom type, of unsigned short int type */
typedef unsigned short int USHRT;

int main()
{
  /* declare variables of the custom data types */
  USHRT num = 16;
  COLORS fingers = (COLORS) BROWN + PINK;

  /* display the variable values */
  printf("values: %d %d\n", fingers, num);

  return 0;
}
```

*Custom data types must be declared in the program before variables of that type can be created – write the declarations before the **main()** function to ensure those types will be available, as in this example.*

Defining constants

The preprocessor directive **#define** can be used to specify constant text values that can be used in the program with this syntax:

#define *CONSTANT-NAME* **"text-string"**

The #define directives are also known as "macro definitions".

Like the **#include** directive, these should appear at the very start of the program code. Any occurrences of the specified constant name in the program code has its associated text string substituted by the compiler before the program is compiled.

The example below defines three string constants with **#define** preprocessor directives and their specified constant names are used in the calls to the **printf()** function. When this program is compiled the compiler first substitutes the text strings in place of the constant names.

Defining text string constants in this way makes the program code much neater and, therefore, more readable.

define.c

The LINE string in this example is just a series of underscore characters.

```
#include <stdio.h>
#define LINE "_____ "
#define TITLE "C Programming in easy steps"
#define AUTHOR "Mike McGrath"

int main()
{
  printf("\n \t %s \n \t %s \n", LINE, TITLE );
  printf("\t by %s \n \t %s \n ", AUTHOR, LINE );
  return 0;
}
```

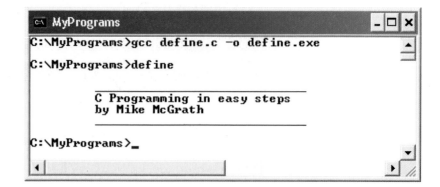

```
C:\MyPrograms>gcc define.c -o define.exe

C:\MyPrograms>define


        C Programming in easy steps
        by Mike McGrath


C:\MyPrograms>_
```

Conditional definitions

A preprocessor "macro" can define a constant according to the result of a test made with an **#if** directive to evaluate an expression. Depending upon the result of this test the macro could then **#define** a constant. The macro must end with an **#endif** directive.

The existence of a constant definition can be tested for with an **#ifdef** directive. This is used in the following example to test for the existence of system constants that are defined by the C compiler itself. A custom constant called **SYS** is then defined as a text string appropriate to the host operating system.

ifmacro.c

```
#include <stdio.h>
#ifdef _WIN32
 #define SYS "Windows"
#endif
#ifdef linux
 #define SYS "Linux"
#endif

int main()
{ printf("Operating system: %s\n", SYS );
  return 0;
}
```

*Compiler-defined constants vary from machine to machine. To discover those on your own system type **cpp -dM file.c** at a prompt, where **file.c** is a valid C file to be compiled. A list of constants will be written out to the screen.*

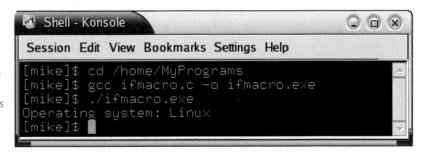

Debugging definitions

Alternatives in an **#if** directive test can be offered with **#else** and **#elif** (else if) directives. This allows conditional branching of the program to run sections of the code according to the test result.

Constants defined with a **#define** directive can be undefined with the **#undef** directive. The **#ifdef** directive, introduced on the previous page, has a companion directive **#ifndef** (if not defined). This can be useful when debugging problem code to hide and unhide sections of the program.

All these preprocessor directives are demonstrated in this example:

debug.c

```
#include <stdio.h>
#define DEBUG 2

int main()
{
  #if DEBUG == 1
    printf("Debug Status is 1\n");
  #elif DEBUG == 2
    printf("Debug Status is 2\n");
  #else
    printf("Default Debug Status\n");
  #endif

  #undef DEBUG

  #ifndef DEBUG
    printf("Debug Status is OFF\n");
  #endif

  return 0;
}
```

The "==" equality operator in this example means "is equal to".

```
MyPrograms

C:\MyPrograms>gcc debug.c -o debug.exe

C:\MyPrograms>debug
Debug Status is 2
Debug Status is OFF

C:\MyPrograms>_
```

Performing operations

All the common C language operators are detailed in this chapter which illustrates, by example, how to perform arithmetical operations, how to assign values and how to make comparisons. The logical operators are explained and demonstrated too, along with the conditional operator.

Covers

Chapter Four

Arithmetical operators

The arithmetical operators commonly used in C programs are listed in the table below together with the operation they perform:

Operator	Operation
+	Addition
-	Subtraction
*	Multiplication
/	Division
%	Modulus
++	Increment
- -	Decrement

The numbers used along with operators to form expressions are called "operands" – in the expression "2+3" the numbers 2 and 3 are the operands.

The operators for addition, subtraction, multiplication and division act as you would expect. Care must be taken, however, to bracket expressions where more than one of these operators is used, to clarify the expression.

```
a = b * c - d % e / f ;        /* this is unclear */

a = (b * c) - ((d % e) / f )   /* this is clearer */
```

The **%** modulus operator will divide the first given number by the second given number and return the remainder of the operation. This is useful to determine if a number has an odd or even value.

The **++** increment operator and **--** decrement operator alter the given value by 1 and return the resulting new value. These are most commonly used to count iterations in a loop. The **++** increment operator increases the value by one while the **--** decrement operator decreases the value by one.

The increment and decrement operators can be placed before or after a value, to different effect. If placed before the operand (prefix), its value is immediately changed, if placed after the operand (postfix) its value is noted first, then the value is changed.

The difference between placing the increment operator before and after an **int** variable operand is demonstrated in this example which illustrates each of the arithmetical operators in action:

arithmetic.c

```c
#include <stdio.h>
int main()
{
    int a=4, b=8, c=1, d=1, result;

    result = a + b;
    printf("Added numbers total %d\n",result);
    result = b - a;
    printf("Subtracted numbers total %d\n",result);
    result = a * b;
    printf("Multiplied numbers total %d\n",result);
    result = b / a;
    printf("Divided numbers total %d\n",result);
    result = a % b;
    printf("Modulus of numbers is %d\n",result);

    printf("Postfix increment is %d\n", c++);
    printf("Now postfix increment is %d\n", c);
    printf("Prefix increment is %d\n",++d);
    printf("Now prefix increment is %d\n",d);

    return 0;
}
```

Notice that the variable value is immediately increased only with the prefix increment operator.

```
MyPrograms

C:\MyPrograms>gcc arithmetic.c -o arithmetic.exe

C:\MyPrograms>arithmetic
Added numbers total 12
Subtracted numbers total 4
Multiplied numbers total 32
Divided numbers total 2
Modulus of numbers is 4
Postfix increment is 1
Now postfix increment is 2
Prefix increment is 2
Now prefix increment is 2

C:\MyPrograms>_
```

Logical operators

The logical operators most commonly used in C programs are listed in the table below:

Operator	Operation
&&	Logical AND
||	Logical OR
!	Logical NOT

The logical operators are used with operands that have the boolean values of true or false, or are values that can convert to true or false.

The logical **&&** AND operator will evaluate two operands and return true only if both operands themselves are true. Otherwise the **&&** operator will return false.

This is used in conditional branching where the direction of a C program is determined by testing two conditions. If both conditions are satisfied the program will go in a certain direction, otherwise it will take a different direction.

Unlike the **&&** operator that needs both operands to be true the **||** OR operator will evaluate its two operands and return true if either one of the operands itself returns true. If neither operand returns true then **||** will return false. This is useful in C programming to perform a certain action if either one of two test conditions has been met.

The third logical operator ! NOT is a unary operator that is used before a single operand. It returns the inverse value of the given operand so if the variable **a** had a value of true then **!a** would have a value of false. The ! operator is useful in C programs to toggle the value of a variable in successive loop iterations with a statement like **a=!a**. This ensures that on each pass the value is changed, like flicking a light switch on and off.

In C programming a zero represents the boolean **false** value and any non-zero value, such as 1, represents the boolean **true** value.

The example below demonstrates how boolean values can be tested with each of the logical operators shown opposite. The ! NOT operator reverses the boolean value, && AND returns 1 if both operands are non-zero values and || OR returns 1 if either operand is a non-zero value.

logic.c

```c
#include <stdio.h>
int main()
{
    int a=1, b=0;

    printf("AND examples:\n");
    printf("\t a && a = %d (true)\n",  a && a );
    printf("\t a && b = %d (false)\n", a && b );
    printf("\t b && b = %d (false)\n", b && b );

    printf("OR examples:\n");
    printf("\t a || a = %d (true)\n",  a || a );
    printf("\t a || b = %d (true)\n",  a || b );
    printf("\t b || b = %d (false)\n", b || b );

    printf("NOT examples:\n");
    printf("\ta = %d !a = %d\n", a, !a );
    printf("\tb = %d !b = %d\n", b, !b );
    return 0;
}
```

Notice that 0 && 0 returns 0, not 1 – demonstrating the anecdote "two wrongs don't make a right".

```
C:\MyPrograms>gcc logic.c -o logic.exe

C:\MyPrograms>logic
AND examples:
        a && a = 1 (true)
        a && b = 0 (false)
        b && b = 0 (false)
OR examples:
        a || a = 1 (true)
        a || b = 1 (true)
        b || b = 0 (false)
NOT examples:
        a = 1 !a = 0
        b = 0 !b = 1

C:\MyPrograms>_
```

Assignment operators

The operators that are used in C programming to assign values are listed in the table below. All except the simple = assign operator are a shorthand form of a longer expression so each equivalent is also given for clarity.

Operator	Example	Equivalent
=	a = b	a = b
+=	a += b	a = a + b
-=	a -= b	a = a - b
*=	a *= b	a = a * b
/=	a /= b	a = a / b
%=	a %= b	a = a % b

It is important to regard the = operator to mean "assign" rather than "equals" to avoid confusion with the == equality operator.

The == equality operator compares operand values and is described on page 48.

In the example above the variable named **a** is assigned the value that is contained in the variable named **b** – so that becomes the new value stored in the **a** variable.

The += operator is useful to add a value onto an existing value that is stored in a variable.

In the table example the += operator first adds the value contained in variable **a** to the value contained in the variable named **b**. It then assigns the result to become the new value stored in the **a** variable.

All the other operators in the table work in the same way by making the arithmetical operation between the two values first, then assigning the result to the first variable to become its new stored value.

With the %= operator the first operand **a** is divided by the second operand **b** then the remainder of the operation is assigned to the **a** variable.

The example program below performs a series of operations to demonstrate each of the assignment operators in action:

assign.c

```c
#include <stdio.h>
int main()
{
  int a, b;

  printf("Assign values example:\n");
  printf("\tVariable a = %d\n", a = 8 );
  printf("\tVariable b = %d\n", b = 4 );

  printf("Add & assign example:\n");
  printf("\tVariable a += b; (8+=4)  a = %d\n", a += b);
  printf("Subtract & assign example:\n");
  printf("\tVariable a -= b; (12-=4) a = %d\n", a -= b);
  printf("Multiply & assign example:\n");
  printf("\tVariable a *= b; (8*=4)  a = %d\n", a *= b);
  printf("Divide & assign example:\n");
  printf("\tVariable a /= b; (32/=4) a = %d\n", a /= b);
  printf("Modulus & assign example:\n\t");
  printf("Variable a %%= b; (8%%=4)  a = %d\n", a %= b);

  return 0;
}
```

*Notice that %% must be used in order to display the % character with the **printf()** function.*

```
C:\MyPrograms
C:\MyPrograms>gcc assign.c -o assign.exe

C:\MyPrograms>assign
Assign values example:
        Variable a = 8
        Variable b = 4
Add & assign example:
        Variable a += b; (8+=4)  a = 12
Subtract & assign example:
        Variable a -= b; (12-=4) a = 8
Multiply & assign example:
        Variable a *= b; (8*=4)  a = 32
Divide & assign example:
        Variable a /= b; (32/=4) a = 8
Modulus & assign example:
        Variable a %= b; (8%=4)  a = 0

C:\MyPrograms>_
```

Comparison operators

The operators that are commonly used in C programming to compare two numerical values are listed in the table below:

Operator	Comparative Test
==	Equality
!=	Inequality
>	Greater than
<	Less than
>=	Greater than or equal to
<=	Less than or equal to

Further information on ASCII codes can be found in the Appendix on pages 162 and 163.

The **==** equality operator compares two operands and will return 1 (true) if both are equal in value, otherwise it will return 0 (false). If both are the same number they are equal, or if both are characters their ASCII code value is compared numerically.

Conversely the **!=** inequality operator returns 1 (true) if two operands are not equal, using the same rules as the **==** equality operator, otherwise it returns 0 (false).

Equality and inequality operators are useful in testing the state of two variables to perform conditional branching in a program.

The **>** "greater than" operator compares two operands and will return 1 (true) if the first is greater in value than the second, or it will return 0 (false) if it is equal or less in value. The **>** "greater than" operator is frequently used to test the value of a countdown value in a loop.

The **<** "less than" operators makes the same comparison but returns 1 (true) if the first operand is less in value than the second, otherwise it returns 0 (false).

Adding the **=** operator after a **>** "greater than" or **<** "less than" operator makes it also return true if the two operands are exactly equal in value.

This example demonstrates each comparison operator in action:

comparison.c

The ASCII code value for uppercase 'A' is 65 and for lowercase 'a' it's 97 – so their comparison in this example returns 0 (false).

```c
#include <stdio.h>
int main()
{
   int a = 0, b = 0, c = 1; char d = 'A', e='a';

printf("Equality example:\n");
printf("\tIs a equal to b? (0==0) %d (true) \n", a==b );
printf("\tIs d equal to e? (A==a) %d (false)\n", d==e );
printf("Inequality example:\n\tIs a not equal to c? ");
printf("(0!=1) %d (true)\n", a != c );
printf("Greater than example:\n\tIs a greater than c?");
printf("(0>1) %d (false) \n", a > c );
printf("Less than example:\n\tIs a less than c? ");
printf("(0<1) %d (true) \n", a < c );
printf("Greater than or equal to example:\n");
printf("\tIs a greater than or equal to b? ");
printf(" (0>=0) %d (true) \n", a >= b );
printf("Less than or equal to example:\n");
printf("\tIs c less than or equal to a? ");
printf("(1<=0) %d (false) \n", c <= a );
return 0;
}
```

```
C:\ MyPrograms                                    _ □ ✕

C:\MyPrograms>gcc comparison.c -o comparison.exe

C:\MyPrograms>comparison
Equality example:
        Is a equal to b? (0==0) 1 (true)
        Is d equal to e? (A==a) 0 (false)
Inequality example:
        Is a not equal to c? (0!=1) 1 (true)
Greater than example:
        Is a greater than c? (0>1) 0 (false)
Less than example:
        Is a less than c? (0<1) 1 (true)
Greater than or equal to example:
        Is a greater than or equal to b?  (0>=0) 1
Less than or equal to example:
        Is c less than or equal to a? (1<=0) 0

C:\MyPrograms>_
```

Conditional operator

Possibly the C programmer's favorite test operator is the **?:** "conditional" operator. This operator first evaluates an expression for a true or false value then executes one of two given statements depending on the result of the evaluation.

The conditional operator has this syntax:

(*test-expression*) ? *if-true-do-this* : *if-false-do-this* ;

This operator is used to execute program statements according to the result of its conditional test. The example below evaluates two integer variable values to determine if they are odd or even numbers. The program outputs an appropriate message according to the result of the test.

conditional.c

```
#include <stdio.h>
int main()
{
 int num1 = 13579, num2 = 24680;
 char letter;

 ( num1 %2 != 0 ) ?
 printf("%d is odd\n",num1): printf("%d is even\n",num2);

 ( num2 %2 != 0 ) ?
 printf("%d is odd\n",num2): printf("%d is even\n",num2);

 letter = ( num2 %2 != 0 ) ? 'Y' : 'N';
 printf("Is %d odd?: %c\n", num2, letter);

 return 0;
}
```

In this example the first two instances of the conditional operator execute the relevant **printf()** function call, whereas the final conditional test assigns the appropriate character value to the **letter** variable.

```
C:\MyPrograms

C:\MyPrograms>conditional.c -o conditional.exe

C:\MyPrograms>conditional
13579 is odd
24680 is even
Is 24680 odd?: N

C:\MyPrograms>_
```

The sizeof operator

The **sizeof** operator returns an integer value that is the number of bytes needed to store the contents of its operand. The operand can be a data type contained inside parentheses, as in the earlier example on page 25, or an expression without parentheses, as seen in the following example. The **sizeof** operator is used here to ascertain the size, in bytes, of various objects in the program:

sizeofop.c

```c
#include <stdio.h>

struct person { char name[50]; int age; float height; };

int main()
{
 int num = 1234567890;
 float dec = 0.123456;
 double ext = 0.0123456789;
 char ltr = 'A';
 char str[] = "Something to write home about...";
 struct person boy;

 printf("Size of num int is %d bytes\n",    sizeof num );
 printf("Size of dec float is %d bytes\n", sizeof dec );
 printf("Size of ext double is %d bytes\n",sizeof ext );
 printf("Size of ltr char is %d byte\n",    sizeof ltr );
 printf("Size of str string is %d bytes\n",sizeof str );
 printf("Size of boy struct is %d bytes\n",sizeof boy );

 return 0;
}
```

*This example includes code for a **struct** object, which is a list of different data type variables. Structs are demonstrated in chapter 10 but the **struct** object is included here to demonstrate that the **sizeof** operator can ascertain the size of a **struct** object.*

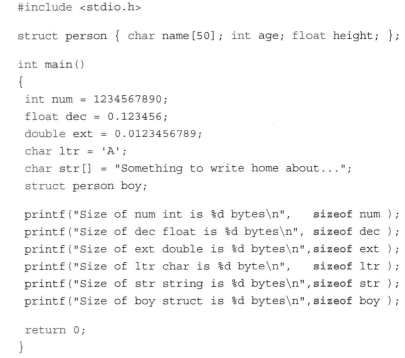

```
C:\MyPrograms>gcc sizeofop.c -o sizeofop.exe

C:\MyPrograms>sizeofop
Size of num int is 4 bytes
Size of dec float is 4 bytes
Size of ext double is 8 bytes
Size of ltr char is 1 byte
Size of str string is 33 bytes
Size of boy struct is 60 bytes

C:\MyPrograms>_
```

Operator precedence

Operator precedence defines the order in which C evaluates expressions. For instance, in the expression a=6+b*3, the order of precedence determines whether the addition or the multiplication is completed first. The table below gives the precedence in decreasing order – operators on the top row have the highest precedence, those on lower rows have successively lower precedence. Operators on the same row have equal precedence.

*The ***** multiply operator is on a higher row than the **+** add operator – so in the expression a=6+b*3 the multiplication is carried out before the addition.*

Operator	Associativity
( ) (function call) **[ ]** (array index) **- >** (struct pointer) **.** (struct member)	Left to right
! (NOT) **~** (bitwise NOT) **++** (increment) **--** (decrement) **+** (positive sign) **sizeof** **-** (negative sign) ***** (pointer) **&** (addressof)	Right to left
* (multiply) **/** (divide) **%** (modulus)	Left to right
+ (add) **-** (subtract)	Left to right
<< (left shift) **>>** (right shift)	Left to right
< (less than) **<=** (less or equal) **>** (greater than) **>=** (greater or equal)	Left to right
= = (equality) **! =** (inequality)	Left to right
& (bitwise AND)	Left to right
^ (bitwise XOR)	Left to right
| (bitwise OR)	Left to right
&& (AND)	Left to right
|| (OR)	Left to right
? : (conditional)	Right to left
= += - = *= /= %= &= ^= |= <<= >>= (all assignment operators)	Right to left
, (comma)	Left to right

The struct operators and bitwise operators appear later in this book but are included here to provide a complete precedence table of all operators.

Making statements

Statements are used in C programming to progress the execution of a program. They may define loops within the code or state expressions to be evaluated. This chapter demonstrates conditional testing and illustrates three different loops.

Covers

Chapter Five

Conditional if statement

The **if** keyword is used to perform the basic conditional test that evaluates a given expression for a boolean value of true or false. Statements following the evaluation will only be executed when the expression is found to be true.

The syntax for the **if** statement looks like this:

if (*test-expression*) { *code-to-be-executed-when-true* }

When the code to be executed is just a single statement the braces may, optionally, be omitted.

The code to be executed may be multiple statements, all contained within the braces, each ending with a semi-colon.

In the example program below the test expression evaluates whether one number is greater than another.

If the first number is, in fact, greater than the second number the expression will be true so the statements inside the braces following the test will be executed.

If the expression was false the statements following the test would not be executed and the program would just move on to the next test, or statement, in the code.

iftest.c

```c
#include <stdio.h>
int main()
{
  if ( 5 > 1 )
  {
    printf("Yes, 5 is greater than 1\n");
    printf("Thanks for asking!\n");
  }
  return 0;
}
```

The test expression in this example could alternatively be if(I < 5) – testing, is I less than 5.

```
C:\ MyPrograms                                    _ □ ✕

C:\MyPrograms>gcc iftest.c -o iftest.exe

C:\MyPrograms>iftest
Yes, 5 is greater than 1
Thanks for asking!

C:\MyPrograms>_
```

Nesting if statements

Conditional **if** statements can be nested inside other **if** statement blocks to test multiple expressions. In this example the three statements calling the **printf()** function will only be executed when all three tested expressions are true.

ifnest.c

Be sure to use the == equality operator to test for equality, rather than the = assignment operator.

```c
#include <stdio.h>
int main()
{
  if ( 5 > 1 )
  {
      if('A'=='A')
      {
          if( 1 != 0 )
          {
            printf("Yes, 5 is greater than 1 \n");
            printf("and A is equal to A \n");
            printf("and 1 does not equal 0 \n");
          }
      }
  }
  return 0;
}
```

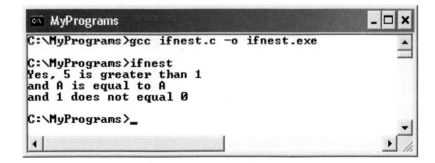

When testing multiple expressions enclose each expression inside parentheses.

An alternative method to evaluate multiple expressions with an **if** statement employs the **&&** logical AND operator. The evaluations in the program listed above could be made in a single test like this:

```c
if( ( 5 > 1 ) && ( 'A'=='A' ) && ( 1 != 0 ) ) { ..... }
```

If-else statement

The **else** keyword can be used with an **if** statement to specify alternative code to be executed in the event that the test expression is false. This is known as "conditional branching" because the program will branch along a certain route according to a test condition. The syntax of an **if-else** statement looks like this:

if (*test-expression*) { *do-this-if-true* } else { *do-this-if-false* }

Several expressions can be tested using successive **else if** statements until a true value is found – whereon the statements following that test will be executed. The following example demonstrates how the **if-else** statement ends after one test is found to be true and its statements have been executed:

ifelse.c

```
#include <stdio.h>
int main()
{
  int num = 2, bool = 0;

  if ( (num == 2) && (bool) )
  {
    printf("The first test is untrue\n");
  }
  else if( (num==2) && (!bool) )
  {
    printf("The second test is true\n");
  }
  else if( (num==2) && (bool==0) )
  {
    printf("The third test is true - but unreached\n");
  }
  return 0;
}
```

*This example uses shorthand for boolean values – (bool) is **true** shorthand for (bool == 1) and (!bool) is **false** shorthand for (bool==0).*

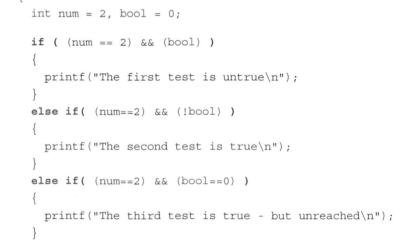

```
MyPrograms

C:\MyPrograms>gcc ifelse.c -o ifelse.exe

C:\MyPrograms>ifelse
The second test is true

C:\MyPrograms>_
```

Switch statement

Conditional branching with long **if-else** statements can often be more efficiently performed using a **switch** statement instead when the test expression just evaluates a single integer.

Each character is represented by the integer value of its ASCII code number – see page 162.

The switch statement works in an unusual way. It takes a given integer value then seeks a matching value among a number of **case** statements.

Code associated with the matching **case** statement will be executed or **default** code may execute if no match is found.

Each case statement must end with a **break** statement to prevent the program continuing through the switch block.

This program gets a single character value from the user then executes the appropriate **case** statement code:

switch.c

```c
#include <stdio.h>
int main()
{
    char letter;
    printf("Enter any single character: ");
    scanf("%c", &letter);

    switch(letter)
    {
        case 'a' : printf("Letter \'a\' found\n"); break;
        case 'b' : printf("Letter \'b\' found\n"); break;
        case 'c' : printf("Letter \'c\' found\n"); break;
        default  : printf("The letter is not a,b or c\n");
    }
    return 0;
}
```

Quotes nested within other quotes must be escaped with the backslash character to avoid confusing the compiler.

```
MyPrograms                                        _ □ ✕
C:\MyPrograms>gcc switch.c -o switch.exe

C:\MyPrograms>switch
Enter any single character: b
Letter 'b' found

C:\MyPrograms>_
```

The for loop

A loop is a piece of code in a program that automatically repeats. One complete execution of all the statements within a loop is called an "iteration", or a "pass".

The length of a loop is controlled by a conditional test made within the loop. While the tested expression is true the loop will continue – until the test expression is found to be false when the loop ends.

In C there are three types of loops – **for** loops, **while** loops and **do-while** loops. Perhaps the most common of these is the **for** loop, which has this syntax:

for (*initializer* ; *test-expression* ; *increment*) { *statements* }

The initializer is used to set a starting value for a counter of the number of iterations made by the loop. An integer variable is used for this purpose and is traditionally named "i".

Alternatively, a **for** *loop counter can count downwards by decrementing the counter value on each pass using i-- instead of i++.*

Upon each iteration of the loop the test-expression is evaluated and that iteration will only continue while this expression is true. When the test-expression becomes false the loop ends immediately without executing the statements again. With every iteration the counter is incremented then the loop's statements are executed.

The example below demonstrates a **for** loop that outputs the number of the current iteration on each pass. When the counter reaches 3 the test-expression becomes false so the loop is terminated. The output is illustrated on the next page together with a further example demonstrating how **for** loops can be nested.

forloop.c

```c
#include <stdio.h>

int main()
{
  int i;

  for( i=0; i < 3; i++ )
  {
    printf("For loop iteration number %d\n", i);
  }
  return 0;
}
```

```
C:\MyPrograms>gcc forloop.c -o forloop.exe

C:\MyPrograms>forloop
For loop iteration number 0
For loop iteration number 1
For loop iteration number 2

C:\MyPrograms>_
```

fornest.c

```c
#include <stdio.h>

int main()
{
    int i,j;

    for( i=1; i < 4; i++)
    {
        printf("Outer loop iteration number %d\n", i);
        for( j=1; j < 4; j++)
        {
            printf("\tInner loop iteration number %d\n", j);
        }
    }
    return 0;
}
```

```
C:\MyPrograms>gcc fornest.c -o fornest.exe

C:\MyPrograms>fornest
Outer loop iteration number 1
        Inner loop iteration number 1
        Inner loop iteration number 2
        Inner loop iteration number 3
Outer loop iteration number 2
        Inner loop iteration number 1
        Inner loop iteration number 2
        Inner loop iteration number 3
Outer loop iteration number 3
        Inner loop iteration number 1
        Inner loop iteration number 2
        Inner loop iteration number 3

C:\MyPrograms>_
```

While loop

Another type of loop uses the **while** keyword followed by an expression to be evaluated for a true or false value.

*Changing the i-- decrementer to an i++ incrementer in this example will create an infinite loop. In this case, on either Windows or Linux systems, press **Ctrl+C** keyboard keys to halt the program.*

If the expression is found to be true then the statements contained within braces following the tested expression will be executed. After the statements have all been executed the test-expression will again be evaluated and the loop will continue until the test-expression is found to be false.

The loop's statement block must contain code that will affect the test-expression in order to change the evaluation result to false, otherwise an infinite loop is created which will lock the system.

Note that if the test expression is found to be false when it is first evaluated the code in the statement block is never executed.

The example below decrements two variable values on each iteration and decrements the counter until it reaches zero – whereon the evaluation is found to be false so the loop ends.

while.c

```c
#include <stdio.h>
int main()
{
   int a=30, b=15, i=3;

   while (i>0)
   {
     a -= 10; b -=5; i--;
     printf("Variable a is %d variable b is %d\n", a,b);
   }
   return 0;
}
```

```
C:\MyPrograms>gcc while.c -o while.exe

C:\MyPrograms>while
Variable a is 20 variable b is 10
Variable a is 10 variable b is 5
Variable a is 0 variable b is 0

C:\MyPrograms>_
```

Do-while loop

The **do-while** loop is a subtle variation of the **while** loop described on the opposite page. In this loop the **do** keyword is followed by a statement block within braces containing all the statements to be executed on each iteration.

The statement block is then followed by the **while** keyword and an expression to be evaluated for a true or false value. If the expression is found to be true the loop continues from the **do** keyword until the test-expression is found to be false – whereon the loop ends.

Note that, unlike the **while** loop, the statements in the **do-while** loop's statement block will always be executed at least once because the test-expression is not encountered until the end of the loop.

The following example will never loop because the counter value is incremented to 1 in the very first execution of the statement block – so the test-expression is found to be false at the first test.

dowhile.c

A *while* loop is often more suitable than a *do-while* loop because its statements are not automatically executed on the first iteration.

```
#include <stdio.h>
int main()
{
   int a=0, i=0;

   do
   {
      ++a;
      ++i;
      printf("Variable a is %d", a);
   }
   while ( i < 1 );

   return 0;
}
```

```
MyPrograms                                    _ □ ✕
C:\MyPrograms>gcc dowhile.c -o dowhile.exe

C:\MyPrograms>dowhile
Variable a is 1
C:\MyPrograms>_
```

Break statement

The **break** keyword was introduced on page 57 to exit individual **case** statements inside a **switch** statement. It has a further important use, however, to exit from any loop.

A **break** statement can be included inside any loop statement block, preceded by a conditional test. When that test is found to be true the **break** statement immediately terminates the loop and no further iterations will be made.

In the following example a **while** loop is set to complete 10 iterations, but when the counter reaches 7 the **break** statement terminates the loop at once.

dobreak.c

A break statement stops a loop instantly – no further iterations are made.

```c
#include <stdio.h>

int main()
{
  int i=0;

  while ( i<10 )
  {
    ++i;
    printf("Loop iteration is %d",i);
    /* if the counter hits 7 end this loop now */
    if( i==7 ) break;
    printf("Go to the next pass\n");
  }
  return 0;
}
```

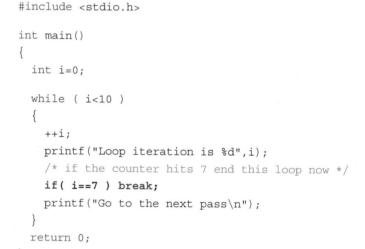

```
C:\MyPrograms>gcc dobreak.c -o dobreak.exe

C:\MyPrograms>dobreak
Loop iteration is 1 - go to the next pass
Loop iteration is 2 - go to the next pass
Loop iteration is 3 - go to the next pass
Loop iteration is 4 - go to the next pass
Loop iteration is 5 - go to the next pass
Loop iteration is 6 - go to the next pass
Loop iteration is 7
C:\MyPrograms>_
```

Continue statement

The C language **continue** keyword can be used to interrupt the execution of a loop but has one important difference to the **break** keyword described opposite – the **continue** keyword only stops the execution of the current iteration of a loop.

Just like in a **break** statement, the **continue** keyword is preceded by a conditional test within the loop's statement block. When its test-expression is found to be true the current iteration is terminated immediately and the next iteration then begins.

Note that the loop counter must be changed before a **continue** test-expression is encountered to avoid creating an infinite loop.

In the following example the test-expression is found to be true when the counter value reaches 3 – so that iteration of the loop is skipped but the loop continues to complete its other passes.

continue.c

```c
#include <stdio.h>
int main()
{
  int i=0;
  while ( i<6 )
  {
    ++i;
    if ( i == 3 ) continue;
    printf("Loop iteration is %d",i);
    printf(" - go to the next pass\n");
  }
  return 0;
}
```

```
C:\ MyPrograms                                    _ □ ✕
C:\MyPrograms>gcc continue.c -o continue.exe
C:\MyPrograms>continue
Loop iteration is 1 - go to the next pass
Loop iteration is 2 - go to the next pass
Loop iteration is 4 - go to the next pass
Loop iteration is 5 - go to the next pass
Loop iteration is 6 - go to the next pass
C:\MyPrograms>_
```

The infamous goto statement

The **goto** keyword supposedly allows the program flow to jump to **labels** at other points in the program, much like a hyperlink on a web page. However, in reality this can cause errors, its use is much-frowned upon and considered bad programming practice.

One possible valid use of the **goto** keyword is to break cleanly from a nested loop. This is demonstrated in the example below which instantly exits both nested loops in the example listed on page 59.

On the whole, though, it should not be used and no other example in this book features the hapless **goto** keyword.

dogoto.c

*The **goto** keyword has existed in computer programs for decades. Its power was abused by many early programmers who created programs that jumped around in an unfathomable manner. This created unreadable programs so the use of **goto** became hugely unpopular, and this remains so today.*

```c
#include <stdio.h>
int main()
{
  int i,j;

  for( i=1; i < 4; i++)
  {
    printf("Outer loop iteration number %d\n", i);
    for( j=1; j < 4; j++)
    {
      if( j==3 ) goto end;      /* jump to label */
      printf("\tInner loop iteration number %d\n", j);
    }
  }

/* label */
  end:
  return 0;
}
```

```
C:\ MyPrograms                                    _ □ ✕
C:\MyPrograms>gcc dogoto.c -o dogoto.exe

C:\MyPrograms>dogoto
Outer loop iteration number 1
        Inner loop iteration number 1
        Inner loop iteration number 2

C:\MyPrograms>_
```

Using functions

In C programming functions contain pieces of code to be executed whenever the function is called in a program. This chapter demonstrates by example a variety of ways that functions can be used in C programs.

Covers

Chapter Six

Function declaration

Previous examples in this book have used the obligatory **main()** function and standard functions contained in the C header library, such as the **printf()** function from the **stdio.h** file. However, most C programs contain a number of custom functions which can be called as required during the execution of the program.

Functions simply contain a group of statements which are executed whenever the function is called. Once their statements have been executed program flow resumes at the point the function was called. This modularity is very useful in programming to separate set routines so they can be used repeatedly.

To introduce a custom function into a program it must first be declared, in a similar manner that variables must be declared before they can be used. Function declarations should be added to the program code before the **main()** function.

Like the **main()** function, custom functions can return a value. The data type of this value must be included in the function declaration. If the function is to return no value its return data type should be declared with the **void** keyword. The function should be named following the same naming conventions used for variable names.

The function prototype is also sometimes referred to as the "function header".

The function declaration is more correctly called the "function prototype" and simply informs the compiler about the function. The actual function definition, which includes the statements to be executed, appears after the **main()** function. The custom function can then be called upon to execute its statements from within the **main()** function, as required.

If a custom function returns a value this can be assigned to a variable of the appropriate data type, or simply displayed as output using the appropriate format specifier.

The following example declares three custom functions called **first()**, **square5()** and **cube5()**.

The **first()** function just outputs a message when called but returns no value. The **square5()** function returns an integer value that is assigned to an **int** variable, whose value is subsequently displayed as output by the **printf()** function. The **cube5()** function also returns an integer value which is directly output by **printf()**.

first.c

Notice that each function prototype must end with a semi-colon.

The custom function definitions could technically appear before the **main()** function without prototypes – but the convention is to include prototypes and keep the **main()** function at the beginning of the program.

```c
#include <stdio.h>

void first();          /* declare function prototypes */
int square5();
int cube5();

int main()                      /* define main function */
{
  int num;
  first();                              /* call function */
  num = square5();                      /* call function */
  printf("5x5= %d\n",num);
  printf("5x5x5= %d\n", cube5() );  /* call function */
  return 0;
}

void first()                   /* define custom function */
{
  printf("Hello from my first() function\n");
}

int square5()                  /* define custom function */
{
  int square = 5*5;
  return square;
}

int cube5()                    /* define custom function */
{
  int cube = (5*5)*5;
  return cube;
}
```

```
MyPrograms

C:\MyPrograms>gcc first.c -o first.exe

C:\MyPrograms>first
Hello from my first() function
5x5= 25
5x5x5= 125

C:\MyPrograms>_
```

Function arguments

Data can be passed as arguments to custom functions who can then use that data in the execution of their statements. The function prototype must include the name and data type of each argument.

Passing data "by value" assigns the value to a variable in the called function – the function can manipulate this copy but it does not affect the original data value.

It is important to recognize that in C programming the data is passed "by value" to the variable specified as the function argument. This is different to some other programming languages, such as Pascal, whose arguments are passed "by reference" – where the function has access to the original data, not just a local copy.

The arguments in a function prototype are known as the "formal parameters" of the function. These may be of different data types and multiple arguments can be specified for a single function if separated by a comma. For example, a function prototype with arguments of each of the four data types could look like this:

```
void action(char c, int i, float f, double d);
```

The argument names used in the function definition can differ from those used in the function prototype but the argument data types, number and order must be the same. It is clearer to adopt the same names in both though.

The compiler checks that the formal parameters specified in the function's prototype match those of the actual function definition and will report an error if they do not match.

The example listed on the opposite page creates three custom functions with one argument each.

The **display()** function has an argument named **str** that is an array of the **char** data type, capable of storing a string of text. Inside the **main()** function a string is assigned to another array named **msg**. When the **display()** function is called, the string in the **msg** variable is passed to the **str** variable, which is then displayed by a call to the **printf()** function.

Both other custom functions, **square()** and **cube()**, have a single argument of the **int** data type. When these functions are called from within the **main()** function an integer value is passed to their argument. This value is used in a piece of arithmetic then the result is returned to the **main()** function. The call to the **square()** function assigns the returned value to an **int** variable – which is subsequently displayed by the **printf()** function. The call to the **cube()** function is itself made from within a call to the **printf()** function so is immediately displayed.

args.c

```c
#include <stdio.h>

void display(char str[]);        /* function prototypes */
int square(int x);
int cube(int y);

int main()                       /* define main function */
{
  char msg[50]= "This string gets passed to a function";
  int num;

  display(msg);                         /* call function */
  num = square(4);                      /* call function */
  printf("4x4= %d\n", num);
  printf("4x4x4= %d\n", cube(4) );  /* call function */
  return 0;
}

void display(char str[])   /* define custom function */
{
  printf("%s\n", str);
}

int square(int x)          /* define custom function */
{
  return (x*x);
}

int cube(int y)            /* define custom function */
{
  return (y*y)*y;
}
```

*A function need not return any value but can include the **return** keyword without any following expression to signify the return of control.*

```
MyPrograms                                           _ □ ✕

C:\MyPrograms>gcc args.c -o args.exe

C:\MyPrograms>args
This string gets passed to a function
4x4= 16
4x4x4= 64

C:\MyPrograms>_
```

Calling other functions

Custom functions can freely call other custom functions, just as readily as they can call standard library functions like **printf()**.

This is demonstrated in the example below that calls a custom function named **getnum()** from within the **main()** function. That function in turn calls another custom function named **square()** during the execution of its statements.

multi.c

```
#include <stdio.h>

void getnum();                    /* function prototypes */
int square(int x);

int main()                        /* define main function */
{
  getnum();                           /* call function */
  printf("End\n");
  return 0;
}

void getnum()                 /* define custom function */
{
  int num;
  printf("Enter an integer to be squared: ");
  scanf("%d", &num);
  printf("%d squared is %d\n", num, square(num) );
}

int square(int x)             /* define custom function */
{
  return (x*x);
}
```

*This example finishes by printing "End" to illustrate that control finally returns to the **main()** function.*

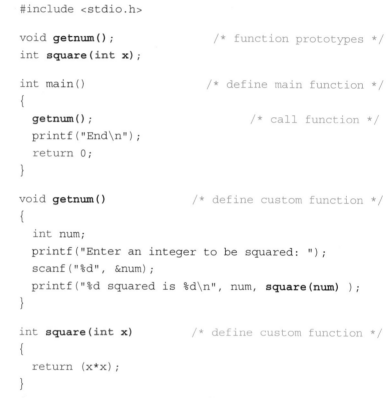

```
C:\MyPrograms>gcc multi.c -o multi.exe

C:\MyPrograms>multi
Enter an integer to be squared: 5
5 squared is 25
End

C:\MyPrograms>_
```

Recursive functions

Functions that call themselves are known as "recursive" functions. As with a loop the function must modify a tested condition to avoid locking the program.

A recursive function is included in the example program listed below. It outputs the current value of a positive integer variable from a starting point entered by the user. That value is decremented with each call of the function until it reaches -1, at which point control is returned to the **main()** function.

recur.c

```c
#include <stdio.h>

void count_down_from(int x);   /* function prototypes */

int main()                         /* define main function */
{
 int num;
 printf("Enter a positive integer to count down from:");
 scanf("%d",&num);
 count_down_from(num);             /* call function */
 return 0;
}

void count_down_from(int x)        /* define function */
{
 printf("%d\n", x);
 --x;
 if( x < 0 ) return;
 else count_down_from(x);          /* call recursively */
}
```

A recursive function can be less efficient than using a loop.

```
MyPrograms
C:\MyPrograms>gcc recur.c -o recur.exe

C:\MyPrograms>recur
Enter a positive integer to count down from: 4
4
3
2
1
0

C:\MyPrograms>_
```

Functions in custom headers

The example programs illustrated throughout this book are necessarily small due to space considerations but in reality most C programs will contain significantly more code.

When developing larger programs some thought should be given to program structure. Maintaining the entire program code in a single file can become unwieldy as the program grows.

Both files are placed in the MyPrograms directory and are compiled with the usual command – the compiler reads the header file automatically because of the #include preprocessor directive.

In order to simplify the program structure a custom header file can be created to contain functions which may be used repeatedly. This should be named with a ".h" file extension, like the standard header files in the C library.

The functions in the custom header file can be made available to the main program file by adding an **#include** preprocessor directive at the beginning of that file. The custom header file name should be enclosed within double quotes though, rather than the < and > angled brackets used to include standard header files.

To illustrate a custom header the program listed on the opposite page builds on the one listed on page 70. The **square()** function has now been removed from the main program and placed in a custom header file named **utils.h**, shown below:

utils.h

```
/* This header file contains utility functions */

int square(int x);        /* function prototype */

int square(int x)         /* function definition */
{
   return (x*x);
}
```

The custom header file function is made available to the program with the **#include "utils.h"** preprocessor directive at the beginning of the program. In this version of the program the user is given the opportunity to complete multiple calculations of square values. Each one is completed by a call to the **square()** function inside the custom header file.

The code within the **main()** function itself is kept to a minimum which indicates an efficient program structure.

square.c

```c
#include <stdio.h>
#include "utils.h"

void getnum();

int main()
{
  getnum();
  printf("End\n");
  return 0;
}

void getnum()
{
  int num;
  char again;
  const char OK='Y', ok = 'y';

  printf("Enter an integer to be squared: ");
  scanf("%d", &num);
  printf("%d squared is %d\n", num, square(num) );

  printf("Square another number?, Y or N:");
  scanf("%1s", &again);

  if( (again==OK) || (again==ok) ) getnum();
  else return;
}
```

*Notice the use of the **%1s** format specifier in this example – this reads the next character entered by the user.*

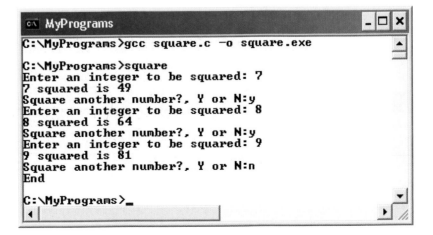

Multiple source files

Programs may comprise multiple source code files to make them more manageable. The following program source code files build on the previous example to allow the user to select an operation from a menu.

The main file calls a function named **menu()** that is in a file named **menu.c**. When the user selects an operation its respective function is called from another file named **ops.c**. The functions that actually perform the arithmetic are located in the **utils.h** custom header file.

Compilation of multiple source code files is slightly different to that used for single files. The technique to compile these programs into a single executable file is demonstrated on page 76.

calc.c

```
#include <stdio.h>

int main()
{
    menu();
    printf("End\n");
    return 0;
}
```

menu.c

```
#include <stdio.h>

void menu();

void menu()
{
    int num;
    printf("\n\tEnter the number of an operation:\n");
    printf("\t1. Square a number\n");
    printf("\t2. Multiply two numbers\n");
    printf("\t3. Exit\n");
    scanf("%d",&num);
    switch(num)
    {
        case 1 : getnum(); break;
        case 2 : getnums(); break;
        case 3 : return;
    }
}
```

If the user selects option 3 control returns to the main() function and the program ends.

ops.c

```c
#include <stdio.h>
#include "utils.h"

void getnum();
void getnums();

void getnum()
{
  int num;
  printf("Enter an integer to be squared: ");
  scanf("%d", &num);
  printf("%d squared is %d\n", num, square(num) );
  menu();
}

void getnums()
{
  int num1, num2;
  printf("Enter 2 numbers to be multiplied, ");
  printf("separated by a space: ");
  scanf("%d", &num1);
  scanf("%d", &num2);
  printf("%dx%d = %d\n",num1,num2,multiply(num1,num2));
  menu();
}
```

*If the user selects menu option 1 or 2 the appropriate function code is executed. Finally the **menu()** function is called once more to again display the options.*

utils.h

```c
/* This header file contains utility functions */

int square(int x);      /* function prototypes */
int multiply(int x, int y);

int square(int x)       /* function definitions */
{
  return (x*x);
}

int multiply(int x, int y)
{
  return (x*y);
}
```

The header file does not need to be compiled itself – its functionality is incorporated into the program by the compiler.

An illustration of this program in action appears on page 77.

Linking files

Although compilers do vary in the way they operate, the process of creating an executable file from source code involves these three basic stages:

- First the preprocessor is called upon to execute all the preprocessor directives. These includes header files, execute macros and carry out any definition substitutions.

- Next the compiler creates a compiled temporary file for each source code file. These are known as object files and normally have the file extension of ".o" or ".obj".

- After creating all the object files the process calls upon an application called a "linker". This is included with each compiler and links together all the object files to create the final single executable program file.

The -c switch means "compile only" and the -o switch means "output as".

The process can be controlled manually using a **-c** switch in the command given to the compiler. This switch tells the compiler to create an object file, but not to call the linker application. For instance, this command creates a compiled object file named **test.o** from a source code file named **test.c**:

gcc -c test.c -o test.o

For programs that have multiple source code files, such as the example on the previous page, individual commands can be issued to create the object files one by one, like this:

calc.o   menu.o   ops.o

gcc -c calc.c -o calc.o
gcc -c menu.c -o menu.o
gcc -c ops.c -o ops.o

Now that the object files are all in place they can be linked together to create the executable program file with this single command:

gcc calc.o menu.o ops.o -o calc.exe

This will then build the file **calc.exe** which can be executed as normal, using the commands **calc** or **calc.exe**, on Windows, and the command **./calc.exe** on Linux.

The illustration on the opposite page shows the compilation process and demonstrates the program in action.

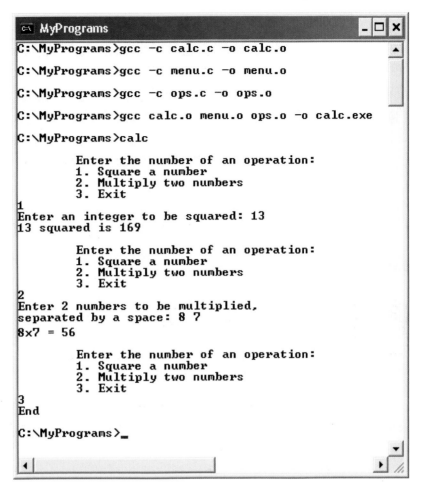

It is a simple matter to enlarge this program because its components are in separate files – add extra menu items to **menu.c**, add extra operations to **ops.c**, add arithmetic functions to the **utils.h** header file.

The GNU C compiler destroys the object files after the executable is created using this method. Other C compilers, such as the Microsoft C compiler may not destroy the object files.

It is worthwhile understanding how the compilation process creates object files that are then linked to create the final executable file.

Typing all these commands is, however, somewhat tedious – especially in large programs that have lots of source code files.

Fortunately, the whole process can be achieved with one single command. For instance, to create the **calc.exe** file in the example illustrated above, type this single command:

gcc calc.c menu.c ops.c -o calc.exe

Static functions

The **static** keyword can be used to restrict the accessibility of functions to the file in which they are created, in exactly the same way that **static** variables have restricted accessibility.

*For more information on **static** variables please refer to page 27.*

To demonstrate this the example below declares and defines a **static** function called **secret()** in the **second.c** file. This can be called by the **call_external()** function located in the same file. Attempting to call the **secret()** function from within the **main.c** file is not permitted and the compiler would not compile that program.

main.c

```
#include <stdio.h>

int main()
{
    printf("Hello from the main file\n");
    call_external();
    return 0;
}
```

second.c

```
#include <stdio.h>

static int secret();

void call_external()
{
    printf("Secret number is %d\n", secret() );
}

static int secret()
{
    return 12345;
}
```

```
MyPrograms                                          _ □ ✕

C:\MyPrograms>gcc main.c second.c -o statfun.exe

C:\MyPrograms>statfun
Hello from the main file
Secret number is 12345

C:\MyPrograms>_
```

Working with bits

This chapter begins by comparing the familiar decimal system to hexadecimal, octal and binary numbering systems. There are examples of binary arithmetic to illustrate the binary system. Bitwise C operators, which work with binary numbers, are described with demonstrations of how to use each operator.

Covers

Chapter Seven

Decimal & hexadecimal

The decimal system

The decimal numbering system, that we use everyday, has a "base" of ten comprising the digits 0 to 9. This probably evolved because we have ten fingers – so it's logical and comfortable to base a numbering system around the value of ten.

For instance, with the number 8,452 we see "eight thousand four hundred and fifty two". This can be expressed as "eight lots of thousands", "four lots of hundreds", "five lots of tens", and "two lots of units", or arithmetically:

```
(8 x 1000) + (4 x 100) + (5 x 10) + (2 x 1) = 8,452
```

Alternatively, this number can be expressed by representing the units, tens, hundreds and thousands as **powers of 10**, like this:

$$(8 \times 10^3) + (4 \times 10^2) + (5 \times 10^1) + (2 \times 10^0) = 8,452$$

Notice how the power value increments from right to left.

The hexadecimal system

Uppercase is commonly used for hexadecimal A, B, C, D, E and F because it appears more readable – lowercase a, b, c, d, e and f would also be valid though.

Unlike the decimal system, hexadecimal has a base number of 16. This system still uses the digits 0 to 9 but also uses the letters A, B, C, D, E and F to represent the decimal numbers 10, 11, 12, 13, 14 and 15 respectively.

For instance, hexadecimal B is the same value as decimal 11.

It is common to clarify the intended numbering system by suffixing the system's base number in subscript – so that 24_{10} indicates the decimal system is being used, whereas 24_{16} indicates the hexadecimal system is being used. With 24_{10} there are two lots of tens and four lots of units, like this:

```
( 2 x 10 ) + ( 4 x 1 ) = 24
```

With 24_{16} there are two lots of sixteen and four lots of units:

```
( 2 x 16 ) + ( 4 x 1 ) = 36 in decimal
```

So 24 in the hexadecimal system is equivalent to decimal 36 and could be expressed like this:

$$(2 \times 16^1) + (4 \times 16^0) = 36$$

The conversion of hexadecimal numbers to decimal requires knowledge of the decimal value of powers of 16, listed in this table:

Also octal numbers have a base value of 8 and can be displayed with the %o format specifier.

Powers of 16	Hexadecimal	Decimal value
16^0	1	1
16^1	10	16
16^2	100	256
16^3	1000	4096
16^4	10000	65536

For instance, the hexadecimal value $112F_{16}$ can be converted as:

```
1 = ( 1 x 16³ ), or ( 1 x 4096)      4096
1 = ( 1 x 16² ), or ( 1 x 256 )       256
2 = ( 2 x 16¹ ), or (  2 x 16 )        32
F = ( 15 x 16⁰ ), or ( 15 x 1 )        15
112F hexadecimal =                   4399 decimal
```

In C programming, hexadecimal numbers are indicated with the prefix "0x" and can be displayed using the format specifier of **%x**, for lowercase representation, or **%X** for uppercase representation.

hex.c

```c
#include <stdio.h>
int main()
{
   printf("%d is %X in hexadecimal", 0x112F, 0x112F);
   return 0;
}
```

```
C:\ MyPrograms                                      _ □ ✕
C:\MyPrograms>gcc hex.c -o hex.exe

C:\MyPrograms>hex
4399 is 112F in hexadecimal
C:\MyPrograms>_
```

Binary numbering

The binary numbering system is the basic numbering system used by computers and has a base of 2. This means that all numbers are represented by just zeros and ones.

Counting up, decimal 1 = binary 1, decimal 2 = binary 10, decimal 3 = binary 11, decimal 4 = binary 100, decimal 5 = binary 101, decimal 6 = binary 110, decimal 7 = binary 111, etc..

To a computer a zero is an "off" state and a one is an "on" state.

The conversion of binary numbers to decimal requires knowledge of the decimal value of powers of 2, listed in this table:

Powers of 2	Binary	Decimal value
2^0	1	1
2^1	10	2
2^2	100	4
2^3	1000	8
2^4	10000	16
2^5	100000	32
2^6	1000000	64
2^7	10000000	128
2^8	100000000	256
2^9	1000000000	512
2^{10}	10000000000	1024
2^{11}	100000000000	2048
2^{12}	1000000000000	4096
2^{13}	10000000000000	8192
2^{14}	100000000000000	16384
2^{15}	1000000000000000	32768
2^{16}	10000000000000000	66536

For instance, the binary value 10110_2 can be converted as:

```
1 = ( 1 x 2⁴ ), or ( 1 x 16 )          16
0 = ( 0 x 2³ ), or ( 0 x 8 )            0
1 = ( 1 x 2² ), or ( 1 x 4 )            4
1 = ( 1 x 2¹ ), or ( 1 x 2 )            2
0 = ( 0 x 2⁰ ), or ( 0 x 1 )            0
10110 binary =                         22 decimal
```

Converting decimal to binary, find the highest power of 2 that will go into a number then do the same with each remainder. For instance, converting decimal 53 to binary:

1×2^5 (32) is the highest power, leaving 21 remaining
1×2^4 (16) is the highest power, leaving 5 remaining
0×2^3 (8) next highest power will not go, so still 5 remaining
1×2^2 (4) is the highest power, leaving 1 remaining
0×2^1 (2) next highest power will not go, so still 1 remaining
1×2^0 (1) is the next highest power

So 110101 binary is equivalent to 53 decimal.

Binary arithmetic works just like decimal arithmetic, for instance:

```
   010
+  111
  1001
```

Binary ASCII code values (listed on page 162/163) are padded with leading zeroes to fill each bit of a byte where necessary. For instance, uppercase 'A' has an ASCII code of 65, which is 1000001 in binary. This is padded to 01000001 to fill all 8 bits of a byte.

Computer memory is measured in bytes. A kilobyte is 1,024 bytes, calculated as 2^{10}. Similarly, a megabyte is 1,048,576 bytes (2^{20}) a gigabyte is 1,073,741,824 bytes (2^{30}), and so on.

At the very basic level each byte comprises 8 bits. A bit is a **B**inary dig**IT** being a single 1 or 0 that forms part of a binary number.

With 8 bits in a byte the binary number in a byte can represent any decimal number in the range of 0 to 255. The significance of this is that all 128 characters defined by standard ASCII codes, plus another 128 special characters, can be stored in computer memory as the binary equivalent of their code number.

This explains why, when a **char** data-type variable is declared in a C program, the machine allocates a byte of memory for storage.

Binary & hexadecimal

Converting from hexadecimal to binary

This is made very simple by virtue of the fact that each number in the range of 0 to 15 (0 to F in hexadecimal) can be represented as a four-bit binary number.

Each binary equivalent for 0 to 15 (0 to F) is listed in this table:

The prefix 0x (zero x) denotes a hexadecimal number.

0 = 0000	4 = 0100	8 = 1000	12 (0xC) = 1100
1 = 0001	5 = 0101	9 = 1001	13 (0xD) = 1101
2 = 0010	6 = 0110	10 (0xA) = 1010	14 (0xE) = 1110
3 = 0011	7 = 0111	11 (0xB) = 1011	15 (0xF) = 1111

To convert any hexadecimal value to binary just replace each individual number with its binary equivalent.

For instance, converting 0x21F to binary:

```
2 = 0010
1 = 0001
F = 1111 (15)
```

So the hexadecimal value 0x21F is binary 001000011111.

Converting from binary to hexadecimal

As with the technique above this process recognizes that each four-bit binary number can represent a hexadecimal value. To convert a binary number to hexadecimal, starting at the right, split it into groups of 4-bit numbers. Then replace each group with its hexadecimal equivalent.

For instance, converting 11010101011 to hexadecimal:

(0)110 1010 1011 - add an initial zero to make the first group of 4

```
0110 = 6
1010 = A
1011 = B
```

So the binary number 11010101011 is hexadecimal 0x6AB.

Bitwise AND operator

The C language has six bitwise operators that can be used to perform calculations with binary digits (bits). To appreciate how they are used it is necessary to understand how to convert decimal numbers to binary numbers, as described on page 83.

Don't confuse the logical **&&** operator with the bitwise **&** operator.

The bitwise **&** AND operator resembles the logical **&&** AND operator inasmuch that it requires two operands. Unlike the **&&** operator, which only returns a value of either 1 or 0, the bitwise **&** operator returns a variety of numbers.

With bitwise **&** AND the operator compares each individual bit of a binary number and returns a 1 or 0 for each comparison. The end result is a series of ones and zeroes that are converted to their decimal number equivalent.

For instance, take the example **13 & 7**. First these decimal operands can be converted to their binary equivalents for bit comparison:

```
13 = 1101 ( (1 x 8) + (1 x 4) + (0 x 2) + (1 x 1) )
7  = 0111 ( (0 x 8) + (1 x 4) + (1 x 2) + (1 x 1) )
```

Starting with the right-hand column each top bit value can now be compared with the corresponding bit value beneath it. If both bits have a value of 1 the **&** AND operator returns 1 for that part of the comparison, otherwise it returns 0 for that part. In this case, both top and bottom bit values in the right-hand column are 1, so the operator returns 1 for that comparison:

The bitwise & comparison only returns a 1 in the resulting bit value when both compared bit values are 1 – a zero and one comparison returns a zero bit value, also comparing two zeros returns a zero bit value.

```
      1101
&     0111
         1
```

The **&** AND operator continues making comparisons across each pair of bit values until it completes those in the left-hand column:

```
      1101
&     0111
      0101
```

Converting the result of this example, 0101, back to decimal reveals that **13 & 7** returns 5 ((0 x 8)+(1 x 4)+(0 x 2)+(1 x 1)).

Bitwise OR operator

Like the bitwise **&** AND operator the bitwise **|** OR operator requires two operands. The **|** OR operator works in a similar way too, but produces a different result.

The | character is commonly known as the "pipe" symbol.

The bitwise **&** operator will only return a bit value of 1 when both operands are themselves 1, whereas the bitwise **|** OR operator will return a bit value of 1 if either operand is 1.

Consequently the bitwise **|** OR operator will only return a bit value of zero when both operands have a value of zero.

For instance, take the example **10 | 9**. First these decimal operands can be converted to their binary equivalents for bit comparison:

```
10 = 1010 ( (1 x 8) + (0 x 4) + (1 x 2) + (0 x 1) )
9  = 1001 ( (1 x 8) + (0 x 4) + (0 x 2) + (1 x 1) )
```

Starting with the right-hand column each top bit value can now be compared with the corresponding bit value beneath it. If both bits have a value of 0 the **|** OR operator returns 0 for that part of the comparison, otherwise it returns 1 for that part. In this case, both top and bottom bit values in the right-hand column are not 0, so the operator returns 1 for that comparison:

```
    1010
|   1001
       1
```

The **|** OR operator continues making comparisons across each pair of bit values until it completes those in the left-hand column:

```
    1010
|   1001
    1011
```

Converting the result of this example, 1011, back to decimal reveals that **10 | 9** returns 11 ((1 x 8)+(0 x 4)+(1 x 2)+(1 x 1)).

The bitwise **|** OR operator should not be confused with the bitwise **^** XOR operator described on the opposite page.

Bitwise **XOR** operator

Like the bitwise **&** AND operator and the bitwise **|** OR operator the bitwise **^** XOR operator (eXclusive OR) also requires two operands. The **^** XOR operator works in a similar way to the **|** OR operator but is subtly different.

The bitwise **|** OR operator will return a bit value of 1 when one or both operands are themselves 1, but the bitwise **^** XOR operator will only return a bit value of 1 if just one operand is 1.

*The **^** character is commonly known as the "hat" symbol – typically found on the 6+shift key.*

Consequently the bitwise **^** XOR operator will return a bit value of zero when both operands have a value of zero, or when both operands have a value of 1.

For instance, take the example **14 ^ 8**. First these decimal operands can be converted to their binary equivalents for bit comparison, like this:

```
14 = 1110 ( (1 x 8) + (1 x 4) + (1 x 2) + (0 x 1) )
8  = 1000 ( (1 x 8) + (0 x 4) + (0 x 2) + (0 x 1) )
```

Starting with the right-hand column each top bit value can now be compared with the corresponding bit value beneath it. If just one bit has a value of 1 the **^** XOR operator returns 1 for that part of the comparison, otherwise it returns 0 for that part. In this case, both top and bottom bit values in the right-hand column are 0, so the operator returns 0 for that comparison:

```
      1110
 ^    1000
      ____
         0
```

The **^** XOR operator continues making comparisons across each pair of bit values until it completes those in the left-hand column:

```
      1110
 ^    1000
      ____
      0110
```

Converting the result of this example, 0110, back to decimal reveals that **14 ^ 8** returns 6 ((0 x 8)+(1 x 4)+(1x 2)+(0 x 1)).

Remember that the "X" in XOR stands for "exclusive", to avoid confusion with the **|** OR operator.

Bitwise NOT operator

The ~ character is called a "tilde", or an "enyay".

Unlike the bitwise **&** AND operator, **|** OR operator and **^** XOR operator the bitwise **~** NOT operator requires just one operand. It converts the value of this single operand to a binary number then reverses each of its bit values – so all ones become zeroes, and all the zeroes become ones. The bitwise ~NOT operator then converts this new binary number to decimal and returns that value.

The value returned by the bitwise ~ NOT operator can best be assigned to a **unsigned short int** variable to be assured that it will be a positive value in the range 0 to 65535.

It is simpler to convert a reversed binary number back to decimal by deducting the original operand value from the possible maximum value of the **unsigned short int** data type, as demonstrated here.

When considering the arithmetic that is performed by the ~ NOT operator it is important to use the full 16-digit binary number. For instance, using the ~NOT operator on a decimal value of 15:

```
 15 = 0000 0000 0000 1111 ( (1x8)+(1x4)+(1x2)+(1x1) )
~15 = 1111 1111 1111 0000 (65535 - 15 = 65520)
```

This ~NOT calculation and those for the previous &AND, | OR and ^ XOR examples are demonstrated in the program below:

bitlogic.c

```c
#include <stdio.h>
int main()
{
    unsigned short int num= ~15, unNOT= ~num;
    printf("num = ~15 = %d, ~num = %d\n", num, unNOT);
    printf("14 ^ 8 = %d\n", 14^8 );
    printf("10 | 9 = %d\n", 10|9 );
    printf("13 & 7 = %d\n", 13&7 );
    return 0;
}
```

```
C:\MyPrograms>gcc bitlogic.c -o bitlogic.exe

C:\MyPrograms>bitlogic
num = ~15 = 65520, ~num = 15
14 ^ 8 = 6
10 | 9 = 11
13 & 7 = 5

C:\MyPrograms>_
```

Setting bit flags

A common use for bitwise operators is to combine several values in a single variable for efficiency. For instance, a program with several "flag" variables, which always have a value of either 1 or 0 (representing true or false states), would normally require eight bits of memory each. The storage of a single digit only requires a single bit, however, so up to eight flags can be combined in a single variable, as seen with the "state" variable in this example:

flags.c

The flag constants have values of increasing powers of 2 to represent individual binary numbers which do not overlap. The state variable value contains an integer total of those flags which are set. For instance, if the state value is 1, flag 1 is set, if the state value is 3, both flags 1 and 2 are set, etc..

```c
#include <stdio.h>
#define FLAG_1      1      /* 0000 0001 */
#define FLAG_2      2      /* 0000 0010 */
#define FLAG_3      4      /* 0000 0100 */
#define FLAG_4      8      /* 0000 1000 */
#define FLAG_5     16      /* 0001 0000 */
#define FLAG_6     32      /* 0010 0000 */
#define FLAG_7     64      /* 0100 0000 */
#define FLAG_8    128      /* 1000 0000 */

int main()
{
    int state = 44;        /* 0010 1100 */
    if ((state & FLAG_1) > 0) printf("Flag 1 is set\n");
    if ((state & FLAG_2) > 0) printf("Flag 2 is set\n");
    if ((state & FLAG_3) > 0) printf("Flag 3 is set\n");
    if ((state & FLAG_4) > 0) printf("Flag 4 is set\n");
    if ((state & FLAG_5) > 0) printf("Flag 5 is set\n");
    if ((state & FLAG_6) > 0) printf("Flag 6 is set\n");
    if ((state & FLAG_7) > 0) printf("Flag 7 is set\n");
    if ((state & FLAG_8) > 0) printf("Flag 8 is set\n");
    return 0;
}
```

```
MyPrograms                                         _ □ ✕
C:\MyPrograms>gcc flags.c -o flags.exe

C:\MyPrograms>flags
Flag 3 is set
Flag 4 is set
Flag 6 is set

C:\MyPrograms>_
```

Bitwise shift operators

Bitwise left-shift operator

The **<<** left-shift operator converts an integer to a binary number then shifts the bits a specified number of places to the left. It fills the vacated bits with zeros then returns the new value as an integer.

The bit at the extreme left of a binary number is referred to as the "most significant bit" and the bit at its extreme right is the "least significant bit".

Bits that are shifted beyond the left limit of the variable container simply fall off the edge and are lost.

The example below begins by shifting the bits one place at a time. Then they are shifted further left so that the significant bit (1) moves to the extreme left of the 16-bit **unsigned short int** variable. The final shift left loses the significant bit altogether.

shiftleft.c

Shifting left has the effect of multiplying the number by 2 for each place shifted.

```c
#include <stdio.h>

int main()
{
    unsigned short int num = 1;   /* 0000 0000 0000 0001 */

    printf("Number is %d\n",num);
    num = num << 1;                   /* 0000 0000 0000 0010 */
    printf("Number is %d\n",num);
    num = num << 1;                   /* 0000 0000 0000 0100 */
    printf("Number is %d\n",num);
    num = num << 13;                  /* 1000 0000 0000 0000 */
    printf("Number is %d\n",num);
    num = num << 1;            /* (1) 0000 0000 0000 0000 */
    printf("Number is %d\n",num);
    return 0;
}
```

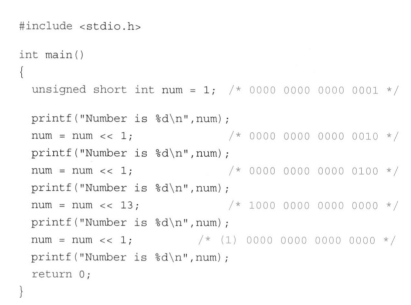

Bitwise right-shift operator

The **>>** right-shift operator converts an integer to a binary number then shifts its bits a specified number of places to the right. It fills the vacated bits with zeros then returns the new value as an integer.

This works like the **<<** left-shift operator but now bits that are shifted beyond the right limit of the variable container fall off the edge and are lost.

The following example shifts the bits right until the significant bit (1) is shifted beyond the extreme right when it becomes lost.

shiftright.c

Shifting right has the effect of dividing the number by 2 for each place shifted.

```c
#include <stdio.h>

int main()
{
  unsigned short int num = 2048;/* 0000 1000 0000 0000 */
  printf("Number is %d\n",num);
  num = num >> 4;              /* 0000 0000 1000 0000 */
  printf("Number is %d\n",num);
  num = num >> 4;              /* 0000 0000 0000 1000 */
  printf("Number is %d\n",num);
  num = num >> 3;              /* 0000 0000 0000 0001 */
  printf("Number is %d\n",num);
  num = num >> 1;           /* 0000 0000 0000 0000 (1)*/
  printf("Number is %d\n",num);
  return 0;
}
```

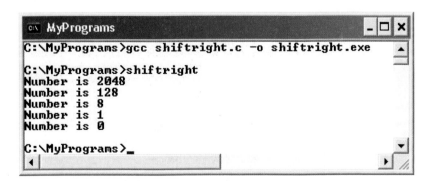

```
C:\MyPrograms>gcc shiftright.c -o shiftright.exe

C:\MyPrograms>shiftright
Number is 2048
Number is 128
Number is 8
Number is 1
Number is 0

C:\MyPrograms>_
```

Extracting bit values

Another use for bitwise operators is to accomplish particular arithmetical tasks. For instance, imagine a 32-bit integer representing a color with 1 byte (8-bits) each for alpha transparency, red, green and blue values. The single value of, say, the red component can be extracted using a bitwise mask, like this:

```
Color:   AAAA AAAA RRRR RRRR GGGG GGGG BBBB BBBB
Mask: &  0000 0000 1111 1111 0000 0000 0000 0000
Result:  0000 0000 RRRR RRRR 0000 0000 0000 0000
```

The zeros in this mask use the bitwise **&** AND operator to ignore all except the red component bits. Binary numbers cannot be used directly in the C code but this mask can be simply stated in hexadecimal form as 0x00FF0000.

The result of this **&** AND operation leaves the red component value followed by trailing zeros from the green and blue values. Using the **>>** right-shift operator to shift the red component 16 places to the right leaves the red component completely isolated.

extract.c

*This example assigns the hexadecimal value of the standard HTML color "indianred" to the variable named **color**. The bitwise operators simply extract the hexadecimal value of the red component from that color.*

```c
#include <stdio.h>
int main()
{
    int color=0x00CD5C5C;
    int mask = 0x00FF0000;

    int red = color & mask;
    red = red >> 16;
    printf("Color indianred is %X\n", color);
    printf("The red component of indianred is %X\n", red);
    return 0;
}
```

```
MyProgrammes                                    _ □ ✕

C:\MyPrograms>gcc extract.c -o extract.exe

C:\MyPrograms>extract
Color indianred is CD5C5C
The red component of indianred is CD

C:\MyPrograms>_
```

Pointing to data

In C programming data can be referenced by pointing to the machine address at which it is stored. This chapter introduces C pointers and demonstrates how they can be used.

Covers

Chapter Eight

The addressof operator

The **&** addressof operator was introduced on page 21 in the example demonstrating how to assign input to a variable with the **scanf()** function. Recall that it must precede the name of the variable name in the call to **scanf()**, as seen in this code fragment:

```
char letter;
scanf("%c", &letter);
```

When a variable is declared, space is reserved in the machine's memory to store data assigned to that variable. The number of bytes reserved depends upon the data type of the variable. The allotted memory is referenced by the unique variable name.

The format specifier for a machine address is %p.

Envisage the computer's memory as a very long row of slots. Each slot has a unique address, which is expressed in hexadecimal format. It's like a long road of houses – each house contains people and has a unique number, in decimal format. In C programs, the houses are slots and the people are the variables.

The **&** addressof operator can be used to return the memory address of any variable in hexadecimal format. The example below displays the machine address of an **int** type variable:

addressof.c

```
#include <stdio.h>
int main()
{
  int num;
  printf("The num variable is at 0x%p\n", &num);
  return 0;
}
```

```
C:\MyPrograms

C:\MyPrograms>gcc addressof.c -o addressof.exe

C:\MyPrograms>addressof
The num variable is at 0x0022FF6C

C:\MyPrograms>_
```

L-values & R-values

Once memory space has been reserved by a variable declaration a value of the appropriate data type can be stored there using the = assignment operator.

For instance, **num=100** takes the value on the right (100) and puts it in the memory referenced by the variable named **num**.

The value to the left of the = assignment operator is known as the "L-value" and the value to its right is known as the "R-value". The "L" in L-value can be considered to mean "location" and the "R" in R-value can be considered to mean "read".

One important rule in C programming is that a R-value cannot appear on the left-hand side of the = assignment operator. On the other hand, a L-value may appear on either side of the = assignment operator. Code that breaks this rule, like the example below, will not be compiled.

values.c

L-values are objects whereas R-values are data.

```
#include <stdio.h>
int main()
{
    int num; char letter; float decimal; double longer;

    /* These are all unacceptable assignment expressions */
    /* R-values cannot appear on the left side of the =  */
    100 = num;
    'A' = letter;
    0.123456 = decimal;
    0.0123456789 = longer;

    return 0;
}
```

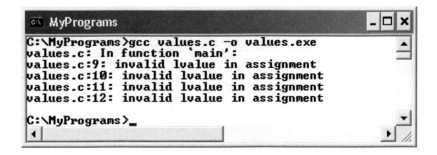

```
C:\MyPrograms>gcc values.c -o values.exe
values.c: In function 'main':
values.c:9: invalid lvalue in assignment
values.c:10: invalid lvalue in assignment
values.c:11: invalid lvalue in assignment
values.c:12: invalid lvalue in assignment

C:\MyPrograms>_
```

Introducing pointers

Pointers are a very useful part of efficient C programming. They are variables that store the memory address of other variables.

Pointer variables are declared in just the same way that other variables are declared but the variable name is prefixed by a "*****". In this case, it represents the "dereference operator", and merely denotes that the declared variable is a pointer. The pointer's data type must match the data type of the variable it points to.

Declare variables before making other statements – for instance, at the beginning of **main()**.

Once declared, a pointer variable can be assigned the address of another variable using the **&** addressof operator. The variable name should not be prefixed by the ***** dereference operator in the assignment statement unless the pointer is initialized immediately in the variable declaration itself.

- A pointer variable name, when used alone, references a memory address expressed in hexadecimal

The example below declares and initializes a pointer named **x_ptr**. A second pointer, named **y_ptr**, is declared then initialized later.

point.c

```c
#include <stdio.h>
int main()
{
    int x = 8, y = 16;

    int *x_ptr = &x;  /* declare & initialize a pointer */
    int *y_ptr;       /* declare another pointer variable */
    y_ptr = &y;       /* assign an address to this pointer */
    printf("Address of x: 0x%p\n", x_ptr);
    printf("Address of y: 0x%p\n", y_ptr);
    return 0;
}
```

```
C:\ MyPrograms                                    _ □ ✕
C:\MyPrograms>gcc point.c -o point.exe

C:\MyPrograms>point
Address of x: 0x0022FF6C
Address of y: 0x0022FF68

C:\MyPrograms>_
```

Getting values via pointers

When the ★ dereference operator is used in a variable declaration it merely indicates that the variable being declared is a pointer.

However, when a ★ dereference operator appears before a pointer variable elsewhere in a program it references the data stored at the address assigned to that pointer.

- A pointer variable name, when prefixed by the ★ dereference operator, references the data stored at the address assigned to that pointer

This means a program can get the address assigned to a pointer variable just by using its name, or it can get the data stored at that address by prefixing its name with the ★ dereference operator.

The example below builds on the previous example to reveal the data stored at the address assigned to each pointer variable:

deref.c

The ★ dereference operator is alternatively known as the "indirection" operator.

```c
#include <stdio.h>
int main()
{
    int x = 8, y = 16;
    int *x_ptr = &x;
    int *y_ptr;
    y_ptr = &y;
    printf("Address of x: 0x%p\n", x_ptr);
    printf("Value of x: %d\n", *x_ptr );
    printf("Address of y: 0x%p\n", y_ptr);
    printf("Value of y: %d\n", *y_ptr );
    return 0;
}
```

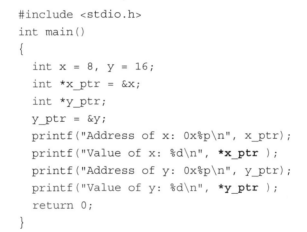

```
C:\MyPrograms

C:\MyPrograms>gcc deref.c -o deref.exe

C:\MyPrograms>deref
Address of x: 0x0022FF6C
Value of x: 8
Address of y: 0x0022FF68
Value of y: 16

C:\MyPrograms>_
```

Pointer arithmetic

Once a pointer variable has been created with an assigned address it can be reassigned another address or moved using arithmetic.

The **++** increment operator and the **--** decrement operator will move the pointer along to the next or previous address for that data type – the larger the data type, the bigger the jump.

Larger jumps can be achieved using the **+=** and **-=** operators.

In the example below the pointer moves up one place, then again by a further one place, before jumping back down two places:

moveptr.c

*The ***=** and **/=** arithmetical operators cannot be used to move a pointer.*

```c
#include <stdio.h>

int main()
{
    int nums[] = {1, 2, 3};

    int *ptr = nums;    /* assign address of 1st element */
    printf("ptr address= %p, value= %d\n", ptr, *ptr);

    ptr++;                  /* move pointer to 2nd element */
    printf("ptr address= %p, value= %d\n", ptr, *ptr);

    ptr++;                  /* move pointer to 3rd element */
    printf("ptr address= %p, value= %d\n", ptr, *ptr);

    ptr-=2;              /* move back down to 1st element */
    printf("ptr address= %p, value= %d\n", ptr, *ptr);

    return 0;
}
```

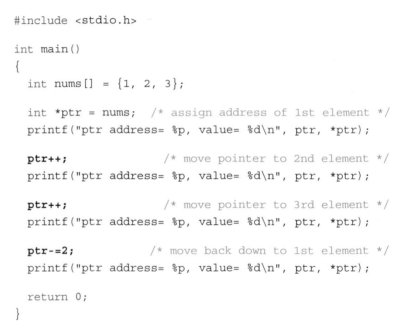

Pointers & arrays

Pointer arithmetic is especially useful with arrays because the elements in an array occupy consecutive memory places.

Assigning just the name of an array to a pointer automatically assigns it the address of the first element. Incrementing the pointer by one moves the pointer along to the next element.

In the following example a pointer is assigned the name of an array called **intArr**, which assigns the address of its first element to the pointer. A loop then increments the pointer to each element.

arrayptr.c

```
#include <stdio.h>

int main()
{
   int intArr[10] = {1,2,3,4,5,6,7,8,9,10};
   int i;
   int *ptr= intArr;          /* shorthand for intArr[0] */

   for (i=0; i<10; i++)
   {
      printf("Element %d value = %d\n", i, *ptr);
      ptr++;
   }
   return 0;
}
```

The name of an array acts like a pointer to its first element.

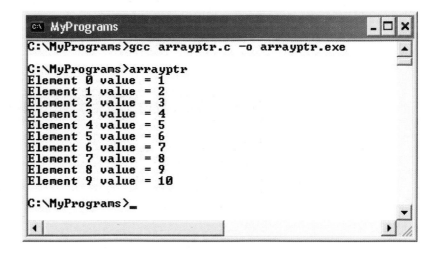

Changing variable values

Besides being able to access the value of a variable via a pointer, a pointer can also be used to change the value inside a variable.

Use the variable pointer name preceded by the ★ dereference operator to assign a new value of the appropriate data type.

In the following example a character array is created with a pointer variable pointing to its first element. The dereferenced pointer is assigned a character which changes the value of the array's first element. The pointer is then moved, using pointer arithmetic, and assigned a character to change the array's fourth element.

modvar.c

Add the \0 null character to the end of an array of characters to promote it to string status.

```c
#include <stdio.h>

int main()
{
  char *ptr;
  char charArr[5] = {'f','i','r','e','\0'};
  ptr= charArr;           /* point to 1st array element */

  printf("String is %s\n", charArr);

  *ptr = 'w';                     /* change 1st element */
  printf("String is %s\n", charArr);

  ptr +=3;                   /* move along 3 elements */

  *ptr = 'y';                     /* change 4th element */
  printf("String is %s\n", charArr);

  return 0;
}
```

```
 MyPrograms                                    _ □ ✕

C:\MyPrograms>gcc modvar.c -o modvar.exe

C:\MyPrograms>modvar
String is fire
String is wire
String is wiry

C:\MyPrograms>_
```

Passing pointers to functions

In C programs function arguments pass their data "by value" to a local variable inside the called function. This means that the function is not operating on the original value, but a copy of it. Passing a pointer to the original value instead overcomes this to allow the called function to operate on the original value.

To demonstrate this, the **main()** function in the example program below creates a local **int** variable, named **num**, together with a pointer to its address. In a call to another function, named **triple()**, the address of the **num** variable is passed to another pointer. Because this second pointer then also points to the **num** variable's address it can be used to assign a new value to **num**.

passptr.c

Notice that the pointer argument must be included in the function prototype declaration.

```c
#include <stdio.h>

void triple(int *ptr);          /* function prototype */

int main()
{
  int num = 5;
  int *ptr = &num;        /* pointer to address of num */

  printf("The num value is %d\n", num);
  triple(ptr);
  printf("The num value is now %d\n", num);
  return 0;
}

void triple(int *number)
{
  *number = (*number * 3);    /* change the num value */
}
```

```
MyPrograms                                    _ □ ✕

C:\MyPrograms>gcc passptr.c -o passptr.exe

C:\MyPrograms>passptr
The num value is 5
The num value is now 15

C:\MyPrograms>_
```

Arrays of pointers

A C program can contain arrays of pointers in which each element of an array contains the address of another variable.

In the example below five pointers contain the address of individual elements of an **int** array. A pointer array called **ptrs** assigns the addresses to its five elements. The address of each of its elements, and the value stored there, is displayed by a **for** loop.

arrintptrs.c

```
#include <stdio.h>
int main()
{
  int intArr[5] = {1,2,3,4,5};     /* an array of ints */

  int *ptr0 = &intArr[0];       /* address of intArr[0] */
  int *ptr1 = &intArr[1];       /* address of intArr[1] */
  int *ptr2 = &intArr[2];       /* address of intArr[2] */
  int *ptr3 = &intArr[3];       /* address of intArr[3] */
  int *ptr4 = &intArr[4];       /* address of intArr[4] */

  /* an array containing all 5 pointers */
  int *ptrs[5] = { ptr0, ptr1, ptr2, ptr3, ptr4 };
  int i;

  for(i=0; i < 5; i++)
  {
  printf("The value at 0x%p is %d\n", ptrs[i], *ptrs[i]);
  }
  return 0;
}
```

Notice how the value of the counter "i" is substituted for the element index number on each iteration of the loop.

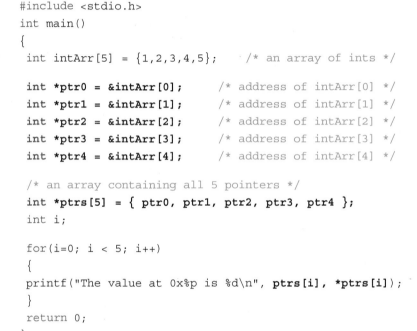

```
C:\MyPrograms>gcc arrintptrs.c -o arrintptrs.exe

C:\MyPrograms>arrintptrs
The value at 0x0022FF48 is 1
The value at 0x0022FF4C is 2
The value at 0x0022FF50 is 3
The value at 0x0022FF54 is 4
The value at 0x0022FF58 is 5

C:\MyPrograms>_
```

A character array that ends with the **\0** null character has string status so can be assigned to a pointer. The name of a string **char** array acts like a pointer to its first element so the addressof operator is not needed when assigning a string to a pointer.

The program below assigns a single string to a **char** pointer and three strings to a **char** pointer array. The address of each element is passed to another function and then their contents are displayed.

strptrs.c

*Notice that the entire string in a **char** pointer is referenced by the pointer name alone – without the * dereference operator.*

```c
#include <stdio.h>

void display(char *ptr[]);        /* function prototype */

int main()
{
    char str[9] = {'C',' ','i','s',' ','f','u','n','\0'};
    char *string = str; /* no addressof operator needed */
    char *strings[3] = { "one","two", "three"};
    printf("%s\n", string);
    display(strings);
    return 0;
}

void display(char *ptr[])          /* function definition */
{
    int i=0;
    while (i<3)
    { printf("%s\n", ptr[i]);
        i++;
    }
}
```

To include a space in a string there must actually be a space between the single quotes, like this ' ' – two single quotes together, such as '' is seen as an empty element and causes a compiler error.

```
C:\MyPrograms

C:\MyPrograms>gcc strptrs.c -o strptrs.exe

C:\MyPrograms>strptrs
C is fun
one
two
three

C:\MyPrograms>_
```

Pointing to functions

Pointers can point to functions, although this ability is used less often than pointers that point to data values.

A pointer to a function is like a pointer to data but must always be enclosed in plain brackets when using the * dereference operator to avoid a compiler error. These will be followed by plain brackets containing any arguments to be passed to the function when using the * dereference operator.

This example contains a pointer to a function named **add()** which takes two arguments and returns an **int** data type. The pointer declaration must match the number of arguments and return type of the function it points at. The function is called, via the pointer, to return the sum total of two integers passed to it as arguments.

fcnptr.c

```
#include <stdio.h>

int add(int x, int y);          /* function prototype */

int main()
{
    int (*ptr)(int x, int y);        /* declare pointer */
    int x=8, y=16;

    ptr = add;            /* point to the add() function */
    /* now call the add() function via the pointer...*/
    printf("%d plus %d equals %d\n", x, y, (*ptr)(x,y) );
    return 0;
}

int add(int x, int y)          /* function definition */
{
    return x+y;
}
```

*Working with pointers takes a little practice – a pointer contains an address, and dereferencing a pointer will access the data value stored at that address. However, an entire string value in a **char** pointer can be referenced using just the pointer name alone.*

```
C:\MyPrograms
C:\MyPrograms>gcc fcnptr.c -o fcnptr.exe

C:\MyPrograms>fcnptr
8 plus 16 equals 24

C:\MyPrograms>_
```

Manipulating strings

This chapter explores the use of text strings in C programming. It demonstrates how a program can use text strings stored in variables and those text strings which are input by a user. Examples illustrate how the standard C string-handling functions can be used to manipulate text strings.

Covers

Chapter Nine

What is a string ?

A string of text is a series of characters, usually forming words. In C programming each character has a unique ASCII code value, including punctuation and non-printing characters such as newline and tab. These are used by C to treat characters numerically. For instance, characters can be changed arithmetically like this:

Refer to page 162 to see the standard ASCII character code table.

```
char letter = 'S';
letter++;        /* changes the letter to 'T' */
```

The ASCII code values for lowercase letters are always 32 higher than those of uppercase letters, so the case of a character can be changed by adding or subtracting a value of 32:

```
char letter = 'A';
letter += 32;  /* changes the letter to 'a' */
letter -= 32;  /* changes the letter back to 'A' */
```

In C, character values must be enclosed by single quotes – strings must be enclosed by double quotes.

C does not have a dedicated **string** data type, but relies instead upon its **char** data type to store strings as character arrays. A **char** array to store a string is declared like this:

```
char arr[6];
```

This declaration reserves sufficient memory space to store six characters. Filling each of these six array elements with characters does not create a string however – just an array of characters. The crucial requirement to create a string in this array is that the final element must contain the **\0** null character.

The inclusion of a **\0** null character in the final element of a character array promotes the array to string status where the entire array is regarded as a "string constant".

There is an example illustrating the assignment of strings to a **char** array and a **char** pointer on page 103.

In a string constant the name of the array acts as an implied pointer to the entire string of characters, ending with the **\0** null character. The **sizeof()** function will return the size of the string when passed a string's name as its argument. A string may be assigned to a **char** array or to a **char** pointer, like this:

```
char arr[6] = {'A','l','p','h','a','\0'};
char *ptr = "Beta";
printf("%s\n", arr);     /* outputs "Alpha" */
printf("%s\n", ptr);     /* outputs "Beta" */
```

The problem with scanf()

The **scanf()** function was introduced on page 21 as a means of introducing character input from the user. This function works well for single characters or multiple characters forming a single word. The problem is that **scanf()** stops reading the input when it encounters a single space or when the return key is pressed.

This means that a string sentence cannot be input using **scanf()** – as soon as a space is input the string ends.

To demonstrate this problem the program below asks the user to enter a string containing spaces. The **scanf()** function is used to read the input which it assigns to two **char** arrays. The contents of each array is then displayed to illustrate what **scanf()** actually recorded:

scanfprob.c

```c
#include <stdio.h>

int main()
{
    char arr1[50];
    char arr2[50];

    printf("Enter up to 50 characters, with spaces\n");
    scanf("%s", arr1);
    scanf("%s", arr2);
    printf("Input read into 1st array: %s\n", arr1);
    printf("Input read into 2nd array: %s\n", arr2);
    printf("Everything else has been lost\n");
    return 0;
}
```

A solution to this problem is provided on the next page.

```
MyPrograms                                              _ □ ✕
C:\MyPrograms>gcc scanfprob.c -o scanfprob.exe

C:\MyPrograms>scanfprob
Enter up to 50 characters, with spaces
The moon shone brightly over the silver sea
Input read into 1st array: The
Input read into 2nd array: moon
Everything else has been lost

C:\MyPrograms>_
```

Reading strings

A solution to the **scanf()** problem, described on the previous page, lies with two standard functions located in the **stdio.h** header file.

The first function is named **gets()** and is used to read input from the user. It can then assign the input string to a **char** array specified as its argument. Normally when the return key is pressed a non-printing newline character is input. The **gets()** function replaces this with a **\0** null character to ensure that the **char** array is promoted to string status.

The companion to the **gets()** function is named **puts()**. This function will output a string specified as its argument, and add a newline at the end.

Both **puts()** and **gets()** are demonstrated in the program below which overcomes the problem in the previous example:

getsputs.c

```
#include <stdio.h>

int main()
{
    char arr[50];

    printf("Enter up to 50 characters, with spaces\n");
    gets(arr);

    printf("\nInput read into array was:\n");
    puts(arr);

    return 0;
}
```

If you don't want a newline added after the output use the printf() function instead of puts() to write the output.

```
MyPrograms
C:\MyPrograms>gcc getsputs.c -o getsputs.exe

C:\MyPrograms>getsputs
Enter up to 50 characters, with spaces
The moon shone brightly over the silver sea

Input read into array was:
The moon shone brightly over the silver sea

C:\MyPrograms>_
```

Finding the length of a string

The standard C libraries include a header file named **string.h** that contains special string-handling functions.

To make these available to a program the **string.h** header file must be added with an **#include** directive at the start of the program.

The **string.h** header file contains a function named **strlen()** that can be used to discover the length of a string specified as its argument. The returned integer will be the total number of characters in that string not including the **\0** null character.

In the following example the **strlen()** function returns the number of characters in a string that is entered by the user:

strlen.c

In this example the **gets()** function added a **\0** null character in the 11th element of the array – this is not included in the number returned by **strlen()**.

```c
#include <stdio.h>
#include <string.h>        /* make strlen() available */

int main()
{
   char arr[50];

   printf("Enter up to 50 characters, with spaces\n");
   gets(arr);
   printf("\nInput read into array is:\n");
   puts(arr);
   printf("String length: %d characters\n", strlen(arr));
   printf("Array size: %d bytes\n", sizeof(arr) );
   return 0;
}
```

```
MyPrograms                                              _ □ X
C:\MyPrograms>gcc strlen.c -o strlen.exe

C:\MyPrograms>strlen
Enter up to 50 characters, with spaces
Lots more words

Input read into array is: Lots more words
String length: 15 characters
Array size: 50 bytes

C:\MyPrograms>_
```

Copying strings

The **string.h** header file contains two useful functions to copy strings from one array to another. To make these available to a program the **string.h** header file must be added with an **#include** directive at the start of the program.

The first string copying function is named **strcpy()** and it requires two arguments. The first argument specifies the name of the target array to copy the string into, and the second argument specifies the name of the source array from where the string should be copied:

strcpy(*target-array*, *source-array*);

All characters in the source array are copied to the target array including the **\0** null terminating character. If there are other elements after the null character these also are padded with **\0**s. This ensures that remnants of the original longer second string in this example no longer survive after the first string is copied there:

strcpy.c

Ensure that the target array is of sufficient size to hold all the characters in the string being copied – including its terminating \0 null character.

```
#include <stdio.h>
#include <string.h>        /* make strcpy() available */

int main ()
{
    char string1[50]= "first string of text";
    char string2[50]= "second (longer) string of text";

    /* copy to string 2 the contents of string1 */
    strcpy(string2, string1);

    printf("1st string contains: %s\n", string1);
    printf("2nd string contains: %s\n", string2);
    return 0;
}
```

```
C:\ MyPrograms                                    _ □ ✕
C:\MyPrograms>gcc strcpy.c -o strcpy.exe

C:\MyPrograms>strcpy
1st string contains: first string of text
2nd string contains: first string of text

C:\MyPrograms>_
```

The second string copying function in the **string.h** header file is named **strncpy()**. This is used like the **strcpy()** function but takes a third argument to specify how much of the string to copy.

strncpy(*target-array,* *source-array,* *length***) ;**

The last element in string2 is number 5 – because array index numbering starts at zero, not one.

The string being copied will begin with the first character of the source string but will end at the position specified by this third argument. After the string has been copied any empty elements in the target array will be padded with **\0** null characters. Ensure that the target array is always at least one element larger than the number of characters being copied to ensure that the final element receives a **\0** null character to give the character array string status.

The example below copies a string of five characters into an array of six elements – so **string2[5]** receives a **\0** null character:

strncpy.c

```c
#include <stdio.h>
#include <string.h>          /* make strncpy() available */

int main ()
{
  char string1[]= "To be or not to be?";
  char string2[6];

  /* copy first 5 characters in string1 to string2 */
  strncpy (string2, string1, 5);

  printf("1st string: %s\n", string1);
  printf("2nd string: %s\n", string2);
  return 0;
}
```

Notice that the size of the first array is not specified but is automatically set because the array is initialized in the declaration. Other arrays that are to be initialized after their declaration, say by user input or copying from other arrays, must specify a size in their declaration.

```
C:\MyPrograms>gcc strncpy.c -o strncpy.exe

C:\MyPrograms>strncpy
1st string: To be or not to be?
2nd string: To be

C:\MyPrograms>_
```

MyPrograms

Validating strings

The header file named **ctype.h** contains a range of standard functions that are useful to perform tests on characters. To make these available to a program the **ctype.h** header file must be added with an **#include** directive at the start of the program.

For instance, the **isalpha()** function determines if the tested character is a letter, the **isdigit()** function determines if the tested character is a decimal digit and the **isalnum()** function determines if the tested character is either a letter or a digit.

Each test function returns a non-zero value (not necessarily a 1), if a tested character is as expected but returns a zero if it is not.

These test functions can be used to validate input from a user to check that it conforms to the format expected by the program. In the program below the user is asked to input six digits which are assigned to a **char** array. Each character is tested in turn to verify that it is indeed a digit. When a non-digit is discovered a call to the **printf()** function writes out an appropriate message.

isval.c

Notice how a variable is used as a flag in this example to record the state of validity – it is initialized as true (1) but is set to false (0) when a non-digit is discovered.

The test in this case !isdigit() could alternatively be expressed using the code isdigit==0.

```c
#include <stdio.h>
#include <ctype.h>          /* make char tests available */

int main()
{
    char string[7];
    char *pos[] = {"1st","2nd","3rd","4th","5th","6th"};
    int i, flag = 1;

    puts("Enter any six numbers without any spaces...");
    gets(string);
    for(i=0; i<5; i++)
    {
        if( !isdigit(string[i]) )
        {
            printf("Non-digit found in the %s entry\n",pos[i]);
            flag=0;
        }
    }
    (flag) ? puts("Entry valid") : puts("Entry invalid");
    return 0;
}
```

```
C:\ MyPrograms                                    _ □ ✕
C:\MyPrograms>gcc isval.c -o isval.exe

C:\MyPrograms>isval
Enter any six numbers without any spaces...
123456
Entry valid

C:\MyPrograms>isval
Enter any six numbers without any spaces...
$5%P78
Non-digit found in the 1st entry
Non-digit found in the 3rd entry
Non-digit found in the 4th entry
Entry invalid

C:\MyPrograms>_
```

The **ctype.h** header file also contains functions to test and change character case. This example converts all input to uppercase:

case.c

There are also **islower()** *and* **tolower()** *functions dealing with lowercase characters – the full range of character test functions are given in the appendix on page 173.*

```c
#include <stdio.h>
#include <ctype.h>          /* make char tests available */
int main()
{
  char string[50]; int i;
  puts("Enter some text..."); gets(string);
  for(i=0; i<50; i++)
  {
  if(!isupper(string[i])) string[i]=toupper(string[i]);
  }
  puts(string);
  return 0;
}
```

```
C:\ MyPrograms                                    _ □ ✕
C:\MyPrograms>gcc case.c -o case.exe

C:\MyPrograms>case
Enter some text...
this text is entered entirely in lowercase
THIS TEXT IS ENTERED ENTIRELY IN LOWERCASE

C:\MyPrograms>_
```

Converting strings

The **stdlib.h** header file contains a useful function named **atoi()** that can convert a string to an **int** data type. To make this available to a program the **stdlib.h** header file must be added with an **#include** directive at the start of the program.

The **atoi()** function takes the string to be converted as its single argument. If the string is empty, or if the string's first character is not a number or a minus sign, then **atoi()** will return zero. Otherwise the numeric string will be converted to an **int** data type until **atoi()** encounters a non-numeric character in the string.

When **atoi()** meets a non-numeric character in the string it returns the number so far converted as an **int** data type. The conversion results in the following example demonstrate how **atoi()** performs the conversion until it meets a non-numeric character:

atoi.c

```
#include <stdio.h>
#include <stdlib.h>               /* make atoi() available */

int main()
{
    char string1[] = "246eight10";
    char string2[] = "-65.8";
    char *string3 = "x13579";
    int result;

    result = atoi(string1);
    printf("str1: %d\n", result );
    printf("str2: %d\n", atoi(string2) );
    printf("str3: %d\n", atoi(string3) );
    return 0;
}
```

```
MyPrograms                                          - □ x
C:\MyPrograms>gcc atoi.c -o atoi.exe

C:\MyPrograms>atoi
str1: 246
str2: -65
str3: 0

C:\MyPrograms>_
```

There is also a function named **itoa()** that can be used to convert an **int** data type to a string. This is widely used but is not part of the standard ANSI specification.

The *itoa()* function is very useful but because it is not part of the ANSI standard it may not be supported by all compilers – it is supported by the GNU C compiler used in this book.

This function requires three arguments to specify the number to be converted, the string to which the converted number is to be assigned, and finally the base to be used for the conversion. For instance, a base of 2 converts the number to a string binary.

An ANSI -compliant alternative to the **itoa()** function is the **sprintf()** function that is part of the **stdio.h** header file. It is less powerful because a base value cannot be specified. It too takes three arguments – to specify the string where the conversion is to be stored, a format specifier and the number to be converted. The function returns the number of characters in the converted string.

itoa.c

```c
#include <stdio.h>
#include <stdlib.h>

int main()
{
  char str[4];  int i;

  printf("12 in binary is %s\n",  itoa(12, str, 2));
  printf("12 in hexadecimal is %s\n",itoa(12, str, 16));

  i = sprintf(str, "%x", 255);
  printf("255 in hexadecimal is %s\n",  str);
  printf("sprintf() returns: %d\n", i);
  return 0;
}
```

Unlike the *itoa()* function, *sprintf()* cannot convert to binary because there is no format specifier for binary numbers.

```
C:\ MyPrograms                                    _ □ ✕
C:\MyPrograms>gcc itoa.c -o itoa.exe

C:\MyPrograms>itoa
12 in binary is 1100
12 in hexadecimal is c
255 in hexadecimal is ff
sprintf() returns: 2

C:\MyPrograms>_
```

String concatenation

The combining of two strings into one single string is more precisely known as string "concatenation".

The **string.h** header file contains two functions that can be used to combine strings. To make these available to a program the **string.h** header file must be added with an **#include** directive at the start of the program.

The first of these functions is named **strcat()** and it takes the name of two strings to be concatenated as its two arguments. The string named as its second argument is added to that named as its first argument and then the function returns the combined first string.

It is important to note that the first string must be large enough to accommodate all the characters of the concatenated string to avoid a compiler error.

This example concatenates two strings and displays their total size:

strcat.c

```
#include <stdio.h>
#include <string.h>

int main()
{
    char string1[100] = "A place for everything ";
    char string2[30] = "and everything in its place";
    int numchars;

    numchars = (strlen(string1) + strlen(string2));
    printf("string1 must hold %d characters\n", numchars);
    strcat( string1, string2);
    printf("%s\n", string1);
    return 0;
}
```

The **strlen()** function returns the length of a string *not including* the **\0** null character – in this case the minimum size of **string1** must be 51, not 50.

```
C:\MyPrograms>gcc strcat.c -o strcat.exe

C:\MyPrograms>strcat
string1 must hold 50 characters
A place for everything and everything in its place
```

The second string concatenation function contained in the **string.h** header file is named **strncat()**. It is similar to the **strcat()** function but takes a third argument to specify how many characters of the second string argument should be added to the first string argument.

In the example below the first call to **strncat()** adds the beginning of the second string onto the first string. A second call to the **strncat()** function adds the end of the second string onto the first string.

Notice how the position to begin copying the characters is stated using pointer arithmetic – the name of the string is an implied pointer to its first character, so its name +1 points to its second character, and so on.

strncat.c

```c
#include <stdio.h>
#include <string.h>

int main()
{
    char string1[100] = "The truth is rarely pure ";
    char string2[32] = "and never simple. - Oscar Wilde";

    /* add the first 17 letters of string 2 to string 1 */
    strncat( string1, string2, 17);
    printf("%s\n", string1);

    /* add the last 14 letters of string 2 to string 1 */
    strncat( string1, (string2 + 17), 14);
    printf("%s\n", string1);
    return 0;
}
```

```
C:\MyPrograms
C:\MyPrograms>gcc strncat.c -o strncat.exe

C:\MyPrograms>strncat
The truth is rarely pure and never simple.
The truth is rarely pure and never simple. - Oscar Wilde

C:\MyPrograms>_
```

Finding substrings

A string can be searched to determine if it contains a specified "substring" sequence of characters with a function named **strstr()**. This is part of the **string.h** header file which must be added with an **#include** directive to make this function available.

The **strstr()** function takes two arguments – the first is the string to be searched and the second is the substring to seek. If the substring is not found the function returns a NULL value. When the substring is found the function returns a pointer to the first occurrence of the specified substring within the searched string.

The following example twice calls **strstr()** to search for a substring. The returned pointer in the successful search is used to output the searched string from the point at which it first occurs.

strstr.c

```
#include <stdio.h>
#include <string.h>
int main()
{
    char *string = "The man who makes no mistakes
                        does not usually make anything";

    printf("%s\n", strstr(string, "woman") );
    if( strstr(string, "woman")==NULL )
            printf("\'woman\' not found in string\n");

    printf("%s\n", strstr(string, "ake"));
    if( strstr(string, "ake")!=NULL )
            printf("\'ake\' found in string\n");
    return 0;
}
```

*The substring "ake" actually occurs three times in the searched string – but after the first instance is found, the **strstr()** function just returns a pointer to its first character.*

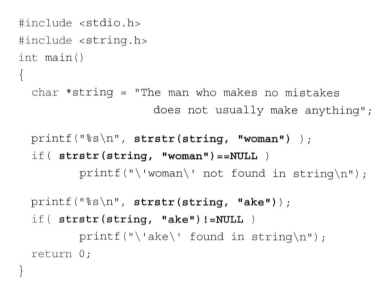

The string position of the first character of a located substring can be calculated using pointer arithmetic – the address of the searched string points to its first character. This can be subtracted from the address of the substring's first character that is returned by the **strstr()** function. The difference reveals the element position of the start of the substring within the searched string.

This calculation is demonstrated in the following program:

strstrpos.c

```c
#include <stdio.h>
#include <string.h>
int main()
{
  char *str = "No time like the present";
  char *sub = "like";
  char *ptr;    /* a pointer for the substring address */
  int   pos;            /* to store the element position */

  ptr = strstr(str,sub); /* get the substring address */

  printf("Address of string \'%s\': 0x%p\n", str, str);
  printf("Address of substring \'%s\': 0x%p\n",sub,ptr);

  pos = (ptr - str);            /* do the arithmetic */

  printf("In decimal, %d - %d = %d\n", ptr, str, pos );
  printf("So the first occurence of %s in\n ", sub);
  printf("\'%s\'\nis at element %d\n", str, pos );
  return 0;
}
```

Element index numbering starts at zero, not one – so element no.8 stores the <u>ninth</u> character.

*The **string.h** header file also contains two functions to search for individual characters. These work just like the **strstr()** function does for substrings. **strchr()** finds the first occurrence of a character in a given string, and **strrchr()** finds its last occurrence – both return NULL if the character is not found.*

```
C:\MyPrograms>gcc strstrpos.c -o strstrpos.exe

C:\MyPrograms>strstrpos
Address of string 'No time like the present': 0x00401280
Address of substring 'like': 0x00401288
In decimal, 4199048 - 4199040 = 8
So the first occurence of like in
 'No time like the present'
is at element 8

C:\MyPrograms>_
```

Comparing strings

In C programming the **==** and **!=** comparison operators cannot be used to compare strings. Instead, the **string.h** header file contains a function named **strcmp()** which can be used for that purpose. To use this function the **string.h** header file must be added with an **#include** directive at the start of the program.

The **strcmp()** function takes the name of two strings to be compared as its two arguments. The comparison is made based upon the numerical value and position of each string character. When the strings are identical **strcmp()** returns zero, otherwise it returns a positive or negative integer depending on the string values. This is demonstrated in the example below which shows that **strcmp()** recognizes that "abc" and "cab" are not identical:

strcmp.c

```
#include <stdio.h>
#include <string.h>
int main()
{
    char *string[4] = {"abc","xyz","cab","abc"} ;
    int result;
    result = strcmp(string[0], string[1]);
    printf("Result comparing abc to xyz is %d\n", result);
    result = strcmp(string[1], string[0]);
    printf("Result comparing xyz to abc is %d\n", result);
    result = strcmp(string[0], string[2]);
    printf("Result comparing abc to cab is %d\n", result);
    result = strcmp(string[0], string[3]);
    printf("Result comparing abc to abc is %d\n", result);
    return 0;
}
```

*The **strcmp()** comparison is case-sensitive – for instance, "ABC" and "abc" are not seen as equal. Comparisons are based on the characters' ASCII values where 'A' is 65 and 'a' is 97 so will not be found equal.*

```
MyPrograms
C:\MyPrograms>gcc strcmp.c -o strcmp.exe

C:\MyPrograms>strcmp
Result comparing abc to xyz is -1
Result comparing xyz to abc is 1
Result comparing abc to cab is -1
Result comparing abc to abc is 0

C:\MyPrograms>_
```

Building structures

In C programming, multiple variables of different data types can be grouped together into structures and unions for convenience. This chapter introduces the **struct** (structure) and **union** abstract data types and demonstrates how they are used.

Covers

Chapter Ten

What is a structure ?

A structure in a C program can contain one, or more, variables of the same, or different data types. These are grouped together in a single structure and can be conveniently referenced using its name.

Grouping related variables together in a structure is helpful in organizing complicated data, especially in large programs. For instance, a structure might be created to describe a payroll record, with variables to store an employee's name, address, salary, national insurance number, etc..

Where arrays can be used to store items of data of the same data type, structures can store items of data of various data types. Each variable in an array is called an "element", but each variable in a structure is called a "member". Individual elements of an array are accessed by their index number (inside square brackets), individual members of a structure are accessed by their given name.

Variable members of a structure cannot be initialized in the declaration.

The "struct" keyword is used to declare a structure in a C program and is followed by an optional "tag" name for that structure. All the variable members of the structure are then listed within a pair of braces – these can include arrays and pointers.

A **struct** containing members to describe the x, y coordinate values of a point in a graph could be declared like this:

*Notice the semi-colon after the **struct** declaration.*

```
struct coords
{
    int x;
    int y;
};
```

The **struct** declaration defines a new data type and variables of that data type can be declared in the same way that **int**, **char**, **float** and **double** variables are declared. For instance, a variable named "point" of the data type "coords" can be declared like this:

*Multiple variables can be declared in a **struct** declaration if separated by a comma – as with regular data types.*

```
struct coords
{
    int x;
    int y;
} point;
```

Each **struct** member can be addressed by appending the "." dot operator and the member's name to the variable name. For instance, the members in the struct declaration above can be addressed as **point.x** and **point.y**.

Typically a struct will be declared in a program before the main() function.

Also, a new **struct** can be declared using the tag name of an existing **struct**. This new **struct** inherits the original member properties. For instance, the declaration below creates a **struct** named "top", based on the **struct** named "coords", with variables **top.x** and **top.y**.

```
struct coords top;
```

The following program demonstrates the examples given above and illustrates how to access the **struct** members:

struct.c

```
#include <stdio.h>

struct coords
{
    int x;
    int y;
} point;

struct coords top;

int main()
{
    point.x = 5; point.y = 8;
    top.x = 16;   top.y = 27;
    printf("point x:%d, point y:%d\n", point.x, point.y);
    printf("top x:%d, top y:%d\n", top.x, top.y);
    return 0;
}
```

```
MyPrograms
C:\MyPrograms>gcc struct.c -o struct.exe

C:\MyPrograms>struct
point x:5, point y:8
top x:16, top y:27

C:\MyPrograms>_
```

Defining type structures

A data type defined by a **struct** can be declared to be a type definition by adding the **typedef** keyword at the beginning of the **struct** declaration. This identifies that **struct** to be a prototype from which other **struct**s can be created simply using any of its declared variable names – without the **struct** keyword.

The program listed below builds on the example given on the previous page to demonstrate how the **struct** named "coords" can be promoted to a type definition. From this two further **struct**s are created using its declared variable named "point". Notice that these **struct** declarations can optionally initialize all their variables as a comma-separated list within braces.

typestruct.c

The **struct** can only assign a list of values to all its variables using this technique in its declaration – not later in the program.

```c
#include <stdio.h>

typedef struct coords
{
    int x;
    int y;
} point;

point top;
point btm = {2,15};

int main()
{
    top.x = 16;
    top.y = 27;
    printf("top x:%d, top y:%d\n", top.x, top.y);
    printf("bottom x:%d bottom y: %d\n", btm.x, btm.y);
    return 0;
}
```

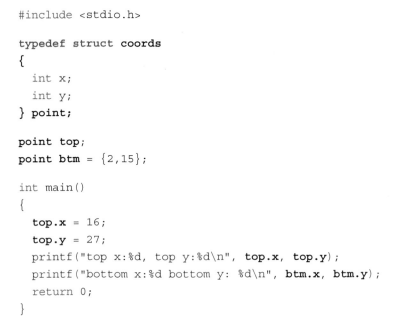

```
C:\MyPrograms>gcc typestruct.c -o typestruct.exe

C:\MyPrograms>typestruct
top x:16, top y:27
bottom x:2 bottom y: 15

C:\MyPrograms>_
```

Nesting structures

A **struct** may be nested inside another **struct**. The example to demonstrate this creates a struct to record the x, y coordinates of two points, representing diagonally opposing corners of a rectangle.

Individual **struct** members are now accessed using two dot operators, following the syntax ***outer-struct.inner-struct.member***.

neststruct.c

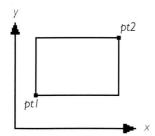

rect box struct *using struct rect box = {5,10,25,25}.*

All four variable values could alternatively be assigned in the declaration of the

```c
#include <stdio.h>

struct coords
{
    int x;
    int y;
};

struct rect
{
    struct coords pt1;
    struct coords pt2;
};

struct rect box;

int main()
{
    box.pt1.x = 5;
    box.pt1.y = 10;
    box.pt2.x = 25;
    box.pt2.y = 25;
    printf("Point 1 x: %d, y: %d\n",box.pt1.x, box.pt1.y);
    printf("Point 2 x: %d, y: %d\n",box.pt2.x, box.pt2.y);
    return 0;
}
```

```
MyPrograms                                    _ □ ✕
C:\MyPrograms>gcc neststruct.c -o neststruct.exe

C:\MyPrograms>neststruct
Point 1 x: 5, y: 10
Point 2 x: 25, y: 25

C:\MyPrograms>_
```

Arrays & pointers in structures

There is an advantage in using a **char** pointer in a **struct** as a string container over using a **char** array for the same purpose.

An entire string can only be assigned to a **char** array when it is declared. The only way to subsequently assign a string to a **struct char** array is one element at a time, because individual elements of the array are **L-value**s. A **char** pointer is also a **L-value** so it can be assigned an entire string after it has been declared.

This example creates a **struct** with both types of **char** members and illustrates the difference in how they may subsequently be assigned string values.

arrvptr.c

```c
#include <stdio.h>

struct example
{
  char arr_string[4];
  char *ptr_string;
} str;

int main()
{
  str.arr_string[0] = 'b';
  str.arr_string[1] = 'a';
  str.arr_string[2] = 'd';
  str.arr_string[3] = '\0';
  str.ptr_string = "good";
  printf("The array string is %s\n", str.arr_string );
  printf("The pointer string is %s\n", str.ptr_string );
  return 0;
}
```

All char array variables are R-values – so cannot appear on the left in an = assignment expression. Their elements, on the other hand, can do because they are L-values.

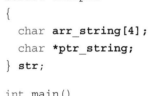

```
C:\MyPrograms>gcc arrvptr.c -o arrvptr.exe

C:\MyPrograms>arrvptr
The array string is bad
The pointer string is good

C:\MyPrograms>_
```

Pointing to structures

Pointers can be created to **struct** data types just as they can with regular data types. The use of pointers to structures is so common in C programs that there is even a special operator to describe it.

In a **struct** pointer the "." dot operator can be replaced by "**->**", which is a hyphen followed by the greater-than character.

The following example demonstrates the creation of a **struct** pointer and illustrates how the **->** arrow operator is used in place of the dot operator:

structptr.c

The -> arrow operator is useful in C programming to differentiate between structure pointers and other pointers.

```c
#include <stdio.h>

typedef struct coords      /* create a point data type */
{
   int x;
   int y;
} point;

int main()
{
   point pt1;            /* create a struct of type point */
   point *pt2;  /* create struct pointer of type point */

   pt1.x = 5;         /* assign values to struct members */
   pt1.y = 10;

   pt2 = &pt1;     /* assign pointer address of struct */

   printf("Starting point %d %d\n",pt1.x, pt2->y );
   printf("Coordinate x: %d, y: %d\n", pt2->x, pt1.y);
   return 0;
}
```

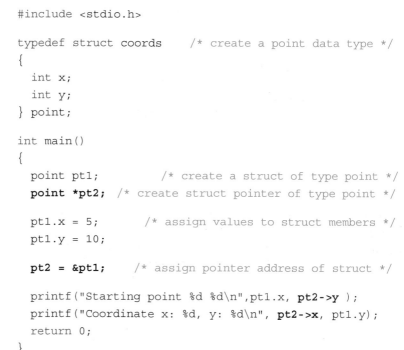

```
C:\MyPrograms>gcc structptr.c -o structptr.exe

C:\MyPrograms>structptr
Starting point 5 10
Coordinate x: 5, y: 10

C:\MyPrograms>
```

s of structures

Structure member values can be stored in an array, just like the values of any other data type.

The array is declared as usual but the method used to assign values to its elements is slightly different. Each comma-separated list of member values must be enclosed by its own pair of braces.

The example below creates an array with three elements of the **point** data type, which contains two members. The array elements are initialized in the declaration with a value given to each member in each element. Subsequently new values are assigned to the members of the third element:

arrstruct.c

```c
#include <stdio.h>

typedef struct coords
{
    int x;
    int y;
} point;

int main()
{
    point pts[3] = { {4,8}, {5,10}, {16,27} };
    pts[2].x = 18;
    pts[2].y = 25;

    printf("Point 0 x: %d, y: %d\n", pts[0].x, pts[0].y );
    printf("Point 1 x: %d, y: %d\n", pts[1].x, pts[1].y );
    printf("Point 2 x: %d, y: %d\n", pts[2].x, pts[2].y );
    return 0;
}
```

Simply assigning all the values as a single comma-separated list will not work – each set of values must be enclosed by its own pair of braces.

```
MyPrograms                                           _ □ ✕

C:\MyPrograms>gcc arrstruct.c -o arrstruct.exe

C:\MyPrograms>arrstruct
Point 0 x: 4, y: 8
Point 1 x: 5, y: 10
Point 2 x: 18, y: 25

C:\MyPrograms>_
```

Passing structures to functions

A structure can be passed as an argument to a function by first specifying the **struct** data type, and a variable name, in the function prototype declaration. Structures of the named type can then be passed to the function named in the prototype declaration. This example passes 2 **point** type **struct**s to a function named **display()**:

passstruct.c

```
#include <stdio.h>

typedef struct coords     /* create a point data type */
{
  int x;
  int y;
} point;

void display( point pt );        /* function prototype */

int main()
{
  point pt1, pt2;     /* create structs of type point */
  pt1.x = 8;                    /* assign member values */
  pt1.y = 16;
  pt2.x = 5;
  pt2.y = 10;

  display( pt1 );           /* pass structs to function */
  display( pt2 );
  return 0;
}

void display( point pt )
{
  printf("Point x: %d, y: %d\n", pt.x, pt.y);
}
```

Pointers to structures can also be passed to functions by first including them in the function prototype declaration. For instance:
void display(point *pt);

```
C:\MyPrograms

C:\MyPrograms>gcc passstruct.c -o passstruct.exe

C:\MyPrograms>passstruct
Point x: 8, y: 16
Point x: 5, y: 10

C:\MyPrograms>_
```

What is a union ?

In C programming a "union" allows different pieces of data, of any data type, to be stored at the same memory locations as the program proceeds – assigning a value to the **union** will overwrite that previously stored there. This allows efficient use of memory.

A **union** is like a **struct** but is declared with the "union" keyword and, because of its nature, its member values can only be assigned individually. This example demonstrates the difference between a **struct** and a **union** and shows how **union** values are overwritten:

union.c
(part of)

It is the programmer's responsibility to understand which type of data is being stored in a union at any point in the execution of the program.

```
#include <stdio.h>

typedef struct data1      /* create a struct of type s */
{
 int num1;
 int num2;
 char letter;
 char *string;
} s;

typedef union data2       /* create a union of type u */
{
  int num1;
  int num2;
  char letter;
  char *string;
} u;

int main()
{
  s sdata = { 10,20,'C',"Programs" };
  u udata;

  /* display value and address of each struct member */
  printf("\nsdata.num1: %d ", sdata.num1 );
  printf("\t\tstored at: 0x%p\n", &sdata.num1 );
  printf("sdata.num2: %d ", sdata.num2 );
  printf("\t\tstored at: 0x%p\n", &sdata.num2 );
  printf("sdata.letter: %c ", sdata.letter );
  printf("\tstored at: 0x%p\n", &sdata.letter );
  printf("sdata.string: %s ", sdata.string );
  printf("\tstored at: 0x%p\n", &sdata.string );
```

union.c
(cont'd)

Unions are mostly useful when memory is very limited.

```c
/* assign a value to each union member in turn then */
/* display value and address of each union member   */

udata.num1 = 8;
printf("\nudata.num1: %d ", udata.num1 );
printf("\t\tstored at: 0x%p\n", &udata.num1 );
udata.num2 = 16;
printf("udata.num2: %d ", udata.num2 );
printf("\t\tstored at: 0x%p\n", &udata.num2 );
udata.letter = 'A';
printf("udata.letter: %c ", udata.letter );
printf("\tstored at: 0x%p\n", &udata.letter );
udata.string = "Union";
printf("udata.string: %s ", udata.string );
printf("\tstored at: 0x%p\n", &udata.string );

/* show the original value is overwritten */
printf("\nudata.num1 is now: %d ", udata.num1 );
printf("- overwritten by \"Union\"\n");

return 0;
}
```

The memory address of each **struct** member is seen to be unique – but the single memory address of the **union** is shared by all its members:

```
C:\MyPrograms>gcc union.c -o union.exe

C:\MyPrograms>union

Struct data num1: 10           stored at: 0x0022FF58
Struct data num2: 20           stored at: 0x0022FF5C
Struct data letter: C          stored at: 0x0022FF60
Struct data string: Programs   stored at: 0x0022FF64

Union data num1: 8             stored at: 0x0022FF54
Union data num2: 16            stored at: 0x0022FF54
Union data letter: A           stored at: 0x0022FF54
Union data string: Union       stored at: 0x0022FF54

Union data num1 is now: 4199245 - overwritten by "Union"

C:\MyPrograms>_
```

Arrays of unions

An array of **union**s can be created in the same way as an array of structures were created in the example on page 128. The difference with **union**s is that its members cannot be initialized in a declaration unless all members are of the same data type. Given the purpose of unions this is unlikely, so each member must be initialized individually by referencing its array index number.

The example below creates an array of three unions which are then individually assigned member values:

arrunion.c

*The data type of the first member in a union is recognized by the compiler as the default type for that union – in this case it's the **char** data type. So the array of unions in this example could be initialized in its declaration with the assignment of =\{"one","two","three"\};*

```
#include <stdio.h>

typedef union data   /* declare union of type uniondata */
{
  char *fname;
  char *lname;
  int age;
} uniondata;

int main()
{
  uniondata toon[3];        /* create an array of unions */
  /* but can't initialize with ={"Mickey","Mouse",75}; */

  toon[0].fname = "Mickey";     /* initialize elements */
  toon[1].lname = "Mouse";
  toon[2].age = 75;

  printf("%s ", toon[0].fname);
  printf("%s ", toon[1].lname);
  printf("is %d years old\n", toon[2].age);
  return 0;
}
```

```
C:\MyPrograms>gcc arrunion.c -o arrunion.exe

C:\MyPrograms>arrunion
Mickey Mouse is 75 years old

C:\MyPrograms>_
```

MyPrograms

Unions in structures

Unions can be declared inside a **struct** definition to allow values of different data types to be stored at the same memory address during the progress of the program. The example below first uses a **union** to store a **char** value which is used in a comparison. Then the **union** is used to store an **int** value which is subsequently displayed in hexadecimal format.

useunion.c

```
#include <stdio.h>

typedef struct
{
  union { int num; char letter; };
  char *name;
} info;

int main()
{
 info stored;       /* create a struct of the info type */
 printf("Please enter your first name: ");
 gets( stored.name );
 printf("Enter a number to convert to hex? [Y or N]: ");
 scanf("%c", &stored.letter );
 if( stored.letter == 'y' || stored.letter =='Y')
 {
   printf("OK, enter the number to be converted: ");
   scanf("%d", &stored.num );
   printf("Thanks %s, ", stored.name );
   printf("%d in hex is 0x%X\n",stored.num,stored.num );
 }
 return 0;
}
```

The hexadecimal numbering system is informally referred to as "hex".

```
C:\MyPrograms>gcc useunion.c -o useunion.exe

C:\MyPrograms>useunion
Please enter your first name: Mike
Enter a number to convert to hex? [ Y or N ]: y
OK, enter the number to be converted: 1024
Thanks Mike, 1024 in hex is 0x400

C:\MyPrograms>_
```

Pointing to unions

A pointer to a **union** can be created in the same manner in which a pointer to a **struct** is created.

The example below defines a union type that can contain an **int**, **char** or **float** value. A **union** and a pointer are declared then various values are assigned to the **union**. Each one is assigned to the regular union then retrieved by the pointer, using the arrow operator.

unionptr.c

Unions can be passed to functions in the same way that structures can be passed to functions – see the example on page 129.

```c
#include <stdio.h>

typedef union
{
  int num;
  char *str;
  float dec;
} info;

int main()
{
  info uniondata;   /* declare union of the info type */
  info *ptr;        /* & union pointer of the info type */
  ptr = &uniondata;   /* now point to the first union */

  uniondata.num = 5;
  printf("The union value is now: %d\n", ptr->num );
  uniondata.str = "five";
  printf("The union value is now: %s\n", ptr->str );
  uniondata.dec = 0.125;
  printf("The union value is now: %f\n", ptr->dec );
  return 0;
}
```

```
C:\MyPrograms

C:\MyPrograms>gcc unionptr.c -o unionptr.exe

C:\MyPrograms>unionptr
The union value is now: 5
The union value is now: five
The union value is now: 0.125000

C:\MyPrograms>_
```

Reading & writing files

This chapter illustrates how C programs can create and modify files. Examples demonstrate how to create new files and show different ways of reading and writing data into those files.

Covers

Chapter Eleven

Creating a file

A special data type for handling files is defined in the **stdio.h** header file. It is called a file pointer and has the syntax **FILE ★**. File pointers are used to open, read, write and close files.

In a C program a file pointer variable called "file_ptr" can be created with this declaration:

```
FILE *file_ptr;
```

A file pointer points to a structure defined in the **stdio.h** header file that contains information about the file. This includes details about the current character and whether the file is being read or written.

Before a file can be read or written it firstly must always be opened using the **fopen()** function. This takes two arguments which specify the name and location of the file, and a "mode" in which to open the file. The **fopen()** function returns a file pointer if successful, or NULL if the file cannot be opened.

The table below lists all the possible file modes that can be specified as the second argument to the **fopen()** function:

File mode	Operation
r	opens an existing text file for reading
w	opens a text file for writing – creates a new file if none exists or opens an existing file and discards all its previous contents
a	appends – opens or creates a text file for writing at the end of the file
r+	opens a text file to read from or write to
w+	opens a text file to write to or read from
a+	opens or creates a text file to read from or write to at the end of the file
Where the mode includes **b** after any of the file modes listed above, the operation relates to a binary file rather than a text file. For instance, **rb** or **w+b**.	

This statement attempts to open a file called "data.txt", for writing only, and assign the returned file pointer to a file pointer variable:

```
FILE *file_ptr;
file_ptr = fopen("data.txt" , "w" );
```

Notice that both file name and file mode arguments must be enclosed by double quotes.

The file pointer variable can be tested for a NULL value to determine if the attempt to open the file was successful – if the file pointer variable contains a NULL value the attempt has failed.

Once a file has been successfully opened it can be read, or added to, or new text can be written in the file, depending on the mode specified in the call to the **fopen()** function. Following this the open file must then always be closed with the **fclose()** function, which takes the file pointer variable as its single argument.

This example creates a new empty text file called "data.txt" in the MyPrograms directory:

newfile.c

```
#include <stdio.h>
int main()
{
   FILE *file_ptr;              /* 1.declare a FILE pointer */
   file_ptr = fopen("data.txt", "w"); /* 2.create file */

   if(file_ptr !=NULL)                        /*3.test*/
   {
     printf("File created\n");
     fclose(file_ptr); /* 4.remember to close the file */
     return 0;
   }
   else{ printf("Unable to create file.\n"); return 1; }
}
```

Notice that this program returns a value of 1 to the system when the attempt to open the file fails – this tells the system that all did not go well.

```
 MyPrograms                                    _ □ ✕

C:\MyPrograms>gcc newfile.c -o newfile.exe

C:\MyPrograms>newfile
File created

C:\MyPrograms>_
```

Standard input & output file streams

Standard input

The **scanf()** function, used in previous examples, is the simplified version of a function named **fscanf()** which requires an input file stream as its first argument. This indicates a source from where a series of characters will be introduced into the program.

In C programming, the file stream named **stdin** represents the keyboard and is the default source for the **scanf()** function. The function call **scanf(...)** is the same as **fscanf(stdin, ...)**.

Standard output

Similarly, the **printf()** function is the simplified version of a function named **fprintf()** which requires an ouput file stream as its first argument. This indicates a destination where a series of characters will be output from the program.

*Another standard output file stream is named **stderr**, which is used to output error messages to the monitor.*

The file stream named **stdout** represents the monitor and is the default source for the **printf()** function. The function call **printf(...)** is the same as **fprintf(stdout, ...)**.

Other standard functions, which have **stdin** or **stdout** as their default file streams, also have equivalents allowing an alternative file stream to be specified. These can be used to read files by specifying a file pointer as an alternative to reading from the **stdin** file stream. They can also be used to write files by specifying a file pointer as an alternative to the **stdout** file stream.

- The **fputc()** function can be used to write to a file stream one character at a time and its companion, **fgetc()**, can be used to read from a file stream one character at a time.

- The **fputs()** function can be used to write to a file stream one line at a time and its companion, **fgets()**, can be used to read from a file stream one line at a time.

- The **fread()** function can be used to read an entire file stream and its partner **fwrite()** can write an entire file stream.

- The **fscanf()** function and the **fprintf()** functions can be used to read and write file streams with strings and numbers.

Each one of these functions is used in the examples in this chapter to demonstrate reading and writing files.

Writing characters

The **fputc()** function can be used to write
one character at a time. It is generally used
through each character element of a **char**
function takes two arguments to specify t
the file pointer of the open file in which t

The loop in the example below ends whe
found in the array element tested on that iteration.

writechars.c

```
#include <stdio.h>
int main()
{
  FILE *file_ptr;              /* 1.declare a FILE pointer */
  char text[50]= {"Text, one character at a time."};
  int i;
  file_ptr = fopen("chars.txt", "w");  /* 2.open file */

  if(file_ptr !=NULL)                          /* 3.test */
  {
    printf("File chars.txt created.\n");
    for(i=0 ; text[i] ; i++)
    {
      fputc( text[i], file_ptr );       /* 4. write text */
    }
    fclose(file_ptr); /* 5.remember to close the file */
    return 0;
  }
  else { printf("Unable to create file.\n"); return 1; }
}
```

*The **fputc()**
function returns
the ASCII code of
the current
character, or a
constant called **EOF** denoting
that the end of the file is
reached.*

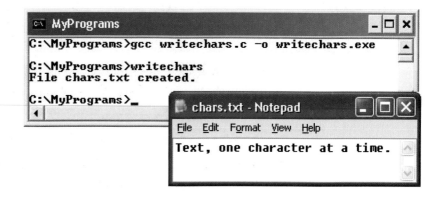

...g characters

The **fgetc()** function can be used to read text from an open text file one character at a time. It is generally used in a loop which moves through each character of the file stream until it encounters the EOF end of file constant. The **fgetc()** function takes a single argument of the file pointer of an open file from which to read.

The example below opens the text file created in the previous example and displays its contents to **stdout** using **printf()**. The loop in this example ends on the iteration where the EOF constant is found in the **char** variable named "next".

readchars.c

```
#include <stdio.h>
int main()
{
  char next;
  FILE *file_ptr;          /* 1.declare a FILE pointer  */
  file_ptr = fopen("chars.txt", "r");  /* 2.open file */

  if( file_ptr !=NULL )                   /* 3.test */
  {
    printf("File chars.txt opened.\nContents: ");
    while(1)
    {
      next = fgetc( file_ptr );          /* 4.read text */
      if(next!=EOF)printf("%c",next);
      else break;
    }
    fclose(file_ptr); /* 5.remember to close the file */
    return 0;
  }
  else { printf("Unable to open file.\n"); return 1; }
}
```

*Note that the conditional test in the **while** loop is simply a 1 (one) – this loop would continue infinitely without the **break** statement.*

```
C:\ MyPrograms                              _ □ ✕
C:\MyPrograms>gcc readchars.c -o readchars.exe  ▲
C:\MyPrograms>readchars
File chars.txt opened.
Contents: Text, one character at a time.
C:\MyPrograms>_                                 ▼
◀                                             ▶
```

Reading lines

The **fgetc()** function is not the most efficient way of reading text into a program because it must be called repeatedly to read each character. It is better to use the **fgets()** function that reads text one line at a time.

The **fgets()** function takes three arguments. The first specifies a **char** pointer, or the name of a sized **char** array, to which the text will be assigned. The second is an **int** specifying the maximum number of characters to read per line. The third is a file pointer specifying where the program will read from.

readlines.c

*This example opens a text file called "more.txt" that contains these three lines of text –
"Line one
Line two
Line three".
Each line is read into the **char** array named text and then written out on each iteration of the **while** loop.*

```c
#include <stdio.h>
int main()
{
  char text[10];
  FILE *file_ptr;              /* 1.declare a FILE pointer  */
  file_ptr = fopen("more.txt", "r");   /* 2.open file */

  if( file_ptr !=NULL )                      /* 3.test */
  {
   printf("File more.txt opened.\nContents:\n");
   while(fgets(text,10,file_ptr)!=NULL)/* 4.read text */
   {
     printf("%s", text);
   }
   fclose(file_ptr);   /* 5.remember to close the file */
   return 0;
  }
  else { printf("Unable to open file.\n"); return 1; }
}
```

```
C:\MyPrograms

C:\MyPrograms>gcc readlines.c -o readlines.exe

C:\MyPrograms>readlines
File more.txt opened.
Contents:
Line one
Line two
Line three
C:\MyPrograms>_
```

Writing lines

The **fputc()** function is not the most efficient method for writing large strings of text because the function is called repeatedly to write each individual character. A better method employs the **fputs()** function that writes the text line by line.

The **fputs()** function takes two arguments that specify a **char** pointer to a string, then a file pointer to the file in which to write. A newline character is added by **fputs()** after the string is written. This function returns zero when successful, or the EOF constant when an error occurs or the end of the file is reached. This example writes the line "Text," then the line "one line at a time.":

writelines.c

The text string need not include a \n newline escape character.

```
#include <stdio.h>
int main()
{
  FILE *file_ptr;            /* 1.declare a FILE pointer */
  char *text = {"Text,\none line at a time."};
  int i;
  file_ptr = fopen("lines.txt", "w");  /* 2.open file */

  if(file_ptr !=NULL)                      /* 3.test */
  {
    printf("File lines.txt created.\n");
    fputs( text, file_ptr );          /* 4. write text */
    fclose(file_ptr); /* 5.remember to close the file */
    return 0;
  }
  else { printf("Unable to create file.\n"); return 1;
}
```

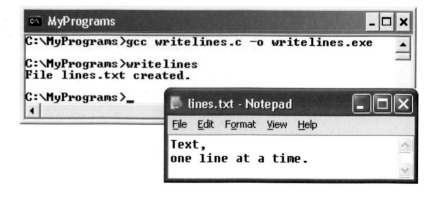

Appending to a file

Specifying a file mode of "a" when opening a file means that any text then written to that file will be added after any existing text.

The program below reopens the text file used by the example on the opposite page. Next the user is asked to enter some text to be appended to the contents of that file. This is assigned to a **char** array by the **gets()** function, that uses the **stdin** file stream by default.

Finally the contents of the char array are appended to the existing contents of the open text file by the **fputs()** function.

append.c

```c
#include <stdio.h>
int main()
{
  char text[50];
  FILE *file_ptr;              /* 1.declare a FILE pointer */
  file_ptr = fopen("lines.txt", "a");  /* 2.open file */

  if( file_ptr != NULL )                    /* 3.test */
  {
    printf("File opened.\nEnter text to append: ");
    gets(text);
    fputs(text, file_ptr);              /* 4. write text */
    fclose(file_ptr); /* 5.remember to close the file */
    return 0;
  }
  else{ printf("Unable to open file.\n"); return 1; }
}
```

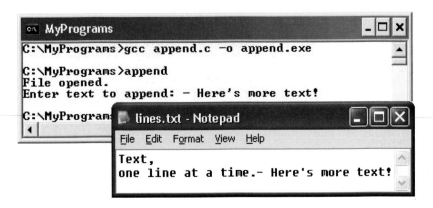

Reading & writing entire files

Whole text files can be read and written with the **fread()** and **fwrite()** functions. Both of these functions take the same four arguments. The first is a **char** variable where the text can be stored. The second argument specifies the size of the chunks of text to read, or write, at a time – normally this will be 1. The third argument specifies the total number of characters to read or write, and the fourth argument is a file pointer to the file to work with.

This example creates a new text file named "dest.txt" and opens a file named "source.txt", whose contents are displayed below:

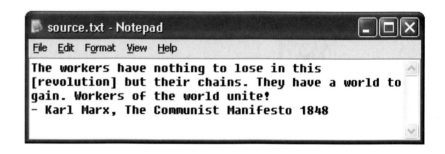

source.txt - Notepad

File   Edit   Format   View   Help

```
The workers have nothing to lose in this
[revolution] but their chains. They have a world to
gain. Workers of the world unite!
- Karl Marx, The Communist Manifesto 1848
```

Use the number returned by fread() *as the third argument to* fwrite() *to ensure that the number of characters read will be the same as those written.*

The **fread()** function assigns the entire text of source.txt to a **char** array named "buffer" and it assigns the sum total number of its characters to an **int** variable named "num".

The **fwrite()** function writes the entire contents of the buffer **char** array into the dest.txt file, shown on the opposite page.

When the copying operation has completed the total number of characters copied is displayed to **stdout** by the **printf()** function.

readwrite.c
(part of)

```c
#include <stdio.h>

int main()
{
    FILE *src_ptr;                  /* 1.declare file pointers */
    FILE *dest_ptr;
    char buffer[1000];
    int num;

    src_ptr  = fopen("source.txt","r"); /* 2.open files */
    dest_ptr = fopen("dest.txt","w");
```

readwrite.c (cont'd.)

*Ensure that the third argument to **fread()** is big enough to allow all the contents to be copied – changing the 1000 value to 100 would make this program only copy the first 100 characters of the text.*

```c
if((src_ptr !=NULL) && (dest_ptr !=NULL)) /* 3.test */
{
  num =fread(buffer,1,1000,src_ptr); /* 4.read text */

  fwrite(buffer, 1, num, dest_ptr); /* 5.write text */

  fclose(src_ptr);/* 6. remember to close the files */
  fclose(dest_ptr);

  printf("Finished: source.txt copied to dest.txt\n");
  printf("%d characters copied\n", num);

  return 0;
}
else
{
  if( src_ptr == NULL)
      printf("Unable to open source.txt\n");
  if( dest_ptr ==NULL)
      printf("Unable to create dest.txt\n");
  return 1;
}
}
```

*The **char** array storing the text must be large enough to accommodate all its characters.*

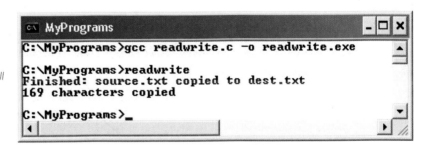

Scanning input

fscanf() takes the same arguments as scanf() plus a first argument that is a file pointer.

The **scanf()** function, used to get user input, is the simplified version of the **fscanf()** function, with its file stream set to **stdin**. It has an advantage when reading files containing just numbers – numbers in a text file are simply seen as string characters, but when read by **fscanf()** they can be converted to their numeric type.

For instance, the program below reads the contents of a text file named "nums.txt". This contains the numbers 1-10, each separated by a space. Because **fscanf()** stops reading when it finds a space, the numbers can easily be assigned to an **int** array.

fscanf.c

```c
#include <stdio.h>
int main()
{
   FILE *file_ptr;
   int nums[30], i, j;

   file_ptr = fopen("nums.txt", "r");
   if(file_ptr !=NULL)
   {
     printf("File nums.txt opened.\n");
     for(i=0; !feof(file_ptr); i++ )
         fscanf(file_ptr, "%d", &nums[i]);
     printf("Total numbers found: %d\n", i);
     printf("Numbers: ");
     for(j=0 ; j<i ; j++) printf("%d ", nums[j]);
     fclose(file_ptr);
     return 0;
   }
   else
   { printf("Unable to open file.\n"); return 1; }
}
```

The function named feof() is used to check for the end of a file – it takes a file pointer as its argument and returns 1 if the end of the file has been reached, or 0 if it hasn't. It is used here to end a loop when the end of the file is encountered.

```
C:\ MyPrograms                                    _ □ ✕
C:\MyPrograms>gcc fscanf.c -o fscanf.exe

C:\MyPrograms>fscanf
File nums.txt opened.
Total numbers found: 10
Numbers: 1 2 3 4 5 6 7 8 9 10
C:\MyPrograms>_
```

Printing output

The **printf()** function, used to write output, is the simplified version of the **fprintf()** function, with its file stream set to **stdout**.

The **fprintf()** function is used just like **printf()** but takes an additional first argument to specify a file stream to write to.

The example below writes a text string to new text file, pointed to by a file pointer variable, then writes the same string to the monitor, indicated by the **stdout** file stream.

fprintf.c

```
#include <stdio.h>
int main()
{
  FILE *file_ptr;
  char *hint= "fscanf() and fprintf() are more flexible
                    \nthan other input/output functions.";

  file_ptr = fopen("hint.txt", "w");

  if(file_ptr !=NULL)
  {
    printf("File hint.txt created\n");
    fprintf( file_ptr, "%s\n", hint );
    fprintf( stdout, "%s\n", hint );
    fclose(file_ptr);
    return 0;
  }
  else { printf("Unable to open file.\n"); return 1;}
}
```

*Unlike other input/output functions the **fscanf()** and **fprintf()** functions provide the ability to use format specifiers.*

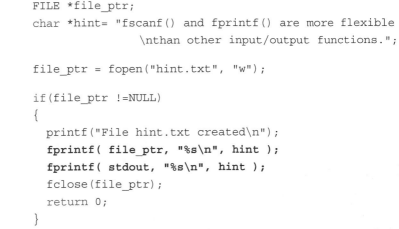

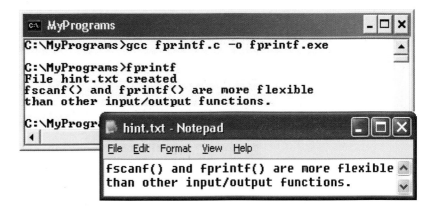

Reporting errors

The C language provides a function named **perror()** in the **stdio.h** header file that can be used to print descriptive error messages. It takes a string as its sole argument to which **perror()** adds a colon followed by a description of a current error.

Also the **errno.h** header file defines an integer expression named "errno" that is assigned an error code number when an error occurs. The **errno** value can be assigned as the argument to a function named **strerror()** to display its associated error message.

The program below demonstrates how **perror()** can be useful to explain an error that occurs when trying to open a missing file. It then continues with a loop displaying a few error code messages.

errno.c

*The range of error code messages associated with the **errno** integer vary from system to system – increase the loop maximum, to say 200, then run this program on your own system to see the full range. Trying this on Windows XP produced 42 messages whereas on Mandrake Linux it produced 124 error messages.*

```c
#include <stdio.h>

int main ()
{
  FILE * file_ptr;
  int i;

  file_ptr = fopen ("nonexistent.file","r");
  if ( file_ptr == NULL ) perror ("Error");
    else fclose (file_ptr);
  printf("\nSome error codes...\n");
  for(i=1; i<6; i++)
    printf("Error %d: %s\n", i, strerror(i) );
  return 0;
}
```

```
MyPrograms                                    _ □ ✕

C:\MyPrograms>gcc errno.c -o errno.exe

C:\MyPrograms>errno
Error: No such file or directory

Some error codes...
Error 1: Operation not permitted
Error 2: No such file or directory
Error 3: No such process
Error 4: Interrupted function call
Error 5: Input/output error
```

Interesting functions

This final chapter explores some of the more interesting standard C functions which have not been examined elsewhere in this book. Examples demonstrate random number generation, date and time functions, and memory management.

Covers

Chapter Twelve

Getting the current date & time

The current time on your system is generally counted as the number of seconds elapsed since 00:00:00 GMT on January 1, 1970 – a point in time known as the "Epoch". The total count represents the current date and time according to the Gregorian calendar and is referred to as "Calendar time".

Remember to #include the time.h header file at the start of the program to make the time functions available.

In C programming the **time.h** header file contains a range of special functions to handle time and date. This includes a function named **time()** that can be used to get the current Calendar time. This is returned as a special data type named **time_t** which is used to point to Calendar time values. The **time()** function requires a single argument which is normally the NULL constant, like this:

```
time_t calendar_time;
calendar_time = time(NULL);
```

Whilst Calendar time may be useful for calculations it is not the way that date and time are normally represented in everyday use. Calendar time can, however, be broken down into a binary representation of year, month, day, hour, and so on. This will also account for time zones to produce a useful local time. The **time.h** header file defines a data type struct named **tm** for the purpose of storing local time, with the components listed in the table below:

*The Daylight Saving component **tm_isdst** is positive if Daylight Saving is in effect, zero if not, and negative if that information is unavailable.*

Component	Description
int tm_sec	seconds after the minute, normally 0 - 59
int tm_min	minutes after the hour, 0 - 59
int tm_hour	hours since midnight, 0 - 23
int tm_mday	day of the month, 1 - 31
int tm_mon	months since January, 0 - 11
int tm_year	years since 1900
int tm_wday	days since Sunday, 0 - 6
int tm_yday	days since January 1st, 0 - 365
int tm_isdst	is Daylight Saving in effect

A function named **localtime()** is used to break down a Calendar time into the components of the **tm** struct. This takes the Calendar time pointed to by a **time_t** data type as its single argument and returns a pointer to a local time.

The components of a local time can be formatted to strings in a number of ways. The simplest method uses a function named **asctime()** to convert the components into a standard format. This requires the local time **tm** struct as its argument.

The program below demonstrates each of these steps and displays both the Calendar time and formatted local time:

timenow.c

```
#include <stdio.h>
#include <time.h>

int main()
{
    /*declare variables for calendar and local time */
    time_t  calendar_time;
    struct tm *local_time;

    /* get the current calendar time. */
    calendar_time = time(NULL);
    printf("%d seconds since the Epoch\n", calendar_time);

    /* convert calendar time to local time */
    local_time = localtime( &calendar_time );

    /* display date and time in the standard format. */
    printf("It's now: %s\n", asctime( local_time ) );
    return 0;
}
```

*Notice that the **& addressof** operator is used in the conversion to local time in order to get the Calendar time from the **time_t** data type.*

```
C:\MyPrograms

C:\MyPrograms>gcc timenow.c -o timenow.exe

C:\MyPrograms>timenow
1131194377 seconds since the Epoch
It's now: Sat Nov 05 12:39:37 2005

C:\MyPrograms>_
```

Specifying date & time formats

Selected local time components can be formatted with the **strftime()** function. This allows special time format specifiers to be applied and works much like the **printf()** and **scanf()** functions. The **strftime()** function takes four arguments to specify a **char** container where the string is to be assigned, the size of the string, the string itself and any format specifiers, and the local time to use.

This example first displays a time in the standard format then selects particular components to be displayed in a specified format:

timefmt.c

A full list of all the time format specifiers is included in the Appendix, on page 183.

```
#include <stdio.h>
#include <time.h>
#define SIZE 256

int main()
{
  char buffer[SIZE];
  time_t  calendar_time;
  struct tm *local_time;
  calendar_time = time(NULL);
  local_time = localtime( &calendar_time );
  printf("It's now: %s\n", asctime( local_time ) );
  strftime (buffer,SIZE,"Day: %A\n",local_time);
  printf("%s",buffer);
  strftime (buffer,SIZE,"Date: %d %B %Y\n", local_time);
  printf("%s",buffer);
  strftime (buffer,SIZE,"Time: %H:%M %p\n",local_time);
  printf("%s",buffer);
  return 0;
}
```

```
C:\MyPrograms                                    _ □ ×
C:\MyPrograms>gcc timefmt.c -o timefmt.exe

C:\MyPrograms>timefmt
It's now: Sat Nov 05 12:55:00 2005

Day: Saturday
Date: 05 November 2005
Time: 12:55 PM

C:\MyPrograms>_
```

Using a timer

Getting the current time both before and after an event means that the duration of the event can be calculated by their difference. The **time.h** header file includes a function named **difftime()** for this particular purpose. The **difftime()** function takes two arguments of **time_t** data types. It subtracts the second argument from the first and returns the difference expressed in seconds, as a **double** type.

The double named "diff" in this example is assigned the time duration of running a loop that makes one billion iterations.

timer.c

```
#include <stdio.h>
#include <time.h>
#define BILLION 1000000000

int main()
{
    time_t start_time, end_time;
    int i;
    float diff;

    printf("Timer started");
    start_time = time(NULL);              /* call 1st time() */
    for( i=0; i < BILLION; i++)           /* run a loop */
        if( i % 100000000 ==0) printf(".");
    end_time = time(NULL);                /* call 2nd time() */
    printf("Timer stopped\n");
    /* calculate the time difference */
    diff = difftime( end_time, start_time );
    printf("It took around %d seconds
                to run the loop\n", (int)diff );
    return 0;
}
```

Each iteration of this loop evaluates an expression that prints a dot when the expression is true, like a progress indicator.

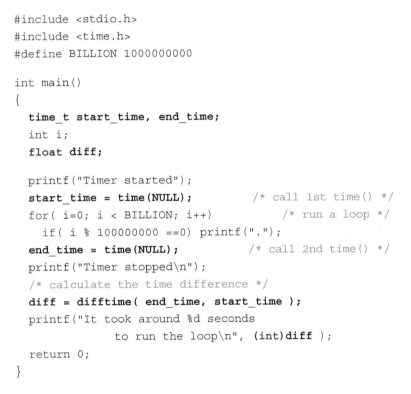

```
C:\MyPrograms>gcc timer.c -o timer.exe

C:\MyPrograms>timer
Timer started.........Timer stopped
It took around 55 seconds to run the loop

C:\MyPrograms>_
```

The time taken to run this loop will vary according to the speed of the system.

Generating random numbers

The **rand()** function generates a "random" positive integer from 0 to a large value (at least 32,767) every time it is called. To set a range for the random numbers use the modulus operator to specify the maximum number. For instance, to set a range from 0 to 9:

```
int r = ( rand() % 9 );
```

To specify a lower limit for the range add it to the result of the expression. For instance, to set a range from 1 to 10:

```
int r = ( rand() % 9) + 1;
```

The numbers generated by **rand()** are not truly random as the function generates the same sequence of numbers each time the program is executed.

In order for **rand()** to generate a different sequence of numbers the seed that starts the sequence must be specified. This is achieved by specifying an integer argument to a function named **srand()**:

```
srand( 12345 );
```

Both *rand()* and *srand()* are part of the **stdio.h** header file – but a program must *#include* the **time.h** header file to make the **time()** function available to set the random seed.

Setting the random seed with **srand()** at the beginning of a program ensures that calls to the **rand()** function will no longer generate the default sequence of numbers. However, although it will now generate a different sequence, it is still one that will be repeated each time the program is executed.

To generate a random sequence the argument to the **srand()** function must be something other than a static integer value. It is commonplace to seed the **rand()** function using the current time as the argument to **srand()**, like this:

```
srand( time(NULL) );
```

Now the sequence of numbers generated by **rand()** will be different on each occasion that the program is executed.

The example program on the opposite page uses the current time to seed the random number generator. It creates an array of integers, in order, from 0 to 49. Random numbers generated by **rand()**, in a range of 1 to 49, are used to shuffle the element values. This means that the array contains all the numbers 1 to 49, in a random order, and without repeating any number.

...cont'd

lotto.c

```c
#include <stdio.h>
#include <time.h>
int main()
{
    int i, r, temp, nums[50];        /* array of numbers */
    srand(time(NULL));   /* seed random number generator */

    for (i=0; i< 50; i++) nums[i] = i;   /* fill 0 - 49 */

    for (i=1; i< 50; i++)
    {
      r= (rand() % 49)+1; /* randomize positions 1 - 49 */
      temp = nums[i]; nums[i] = nums[r]; nums[r] = temp;
    }

    for(i=0; i< 50; i++)        /* show all element values */
    {
      printf("Elem[%d]:%d  ",i, nums[i]);
      (i % 4 != 0) ? printf("\t") : printf("\n");
    }
    printf("\n\nYour 6 lucky LOTTO numbers are: ");
    for(i=1; i< 7; i++) printf("%d  ",nums[i]);
    return 0;
}
```

The line using the conditional operator in this code is just there to format the output into columns.

Element 0 is assigned the value zero and that element is never shuffled.

```
 MyPrograms                                          _ □ X
C:\MyPrograms>gcc lotto.c -o lotto.exe

C:\MyPrograms>lotto
Elem[0]:0
Elem[1]:32       Elem[2]:25       Elem[3]:8        Elem[4]:4
Elem[5]:12       Elem[6]:47       Elem[7]:45       Elem[8]:14
Elem[9]:10       Elem[10]:26      Elem[11]:35      Elem[12]:9
Elem[13]:30      Elem[14]:31      Elem[15]:24      Elem[16]:15
Elem[17]:44      Elem[18]:38      Elem[19]:43      Elem[20]:23
Elem[21]:28      Elem[22]:21      Elem[23]:49      Elem[24]:48
Elem[25]:39      Elem[26]:7       Elem[27]:2       Elem[28]:19
Elem[29]:5       Elem[30]:13      Elem[31]:27      Elem[32]:34
Elem[33]:46      Elem[34]:17      Elem[35]:33      Elem[36]:20
Elem[37]:29      Elem[38]:41      Elem[39]:16      Elem[40]:11
Elem[41]:42      Elem[42]:18      Elem[43]:36      Elem[44]:22
Elem[45]:1       Elem[46]:6       Elem[47]:3       Elem[48]:40
Elem[49]:37

Your 6 lucky LOTTO numbers are: 32  25  8  4  12  47
C:\MyPrograms>
```

Allocating memory

Memory can be allocated dynamically with the **malloc()** function and released when it is no longer needed using the **free()** function.

The *malloc()* and *free()* functions are part of the *stdlib.h* header file which must be added with an *#include* preprocessor directive to make them available.

The **malloc()** function requires an integer value as its argument to specify how many bytes of memory it should reserve, and it returns a pointer to the allocated space. The **free()** function takes the pointer to the space as its argument. It is good practice to always release memory when it is no longer needed.

The example below demonstrates how **malloc()** can be used to allocate memory space based on a user-specified size:

malloc.c

```c
#include <stdio.h>
#include <stdlib.h>

int main ()
{
    int num, i;
    char * buffer;

    printf ("This program generates a random string\n");
    printf ("How long do you want the string to be? ");
    scanf ("%d", &num);
    /* allocate space 1 byte more than user input */
    buffer = (char*) malloc(num+1);
    for(i=0; i<num; i++) buffer[i]=(rand() % 26) + 'a';
    buffer[num]='\0';
    printf ("Your random string is \'%s\'\n",buffer);
    free (buffer);
    return 0;
}
```

The *malloc()* function naturally returns the size of the number of bytes to reserve as an integer pointer. So when the variable pointer being set is not an *int* data type the return from *malloc()* must be cast to the correct type – as seen in this example.

```
C:\MyPrograms>gcc malloc.c -o malloc.exe

C:\MyPrograms>malloc
This program generates a random string
How long do you want the string to be? 25
Your random string is 'phqghumeaylnlfdxfircvscxg'

C:\MyPrograms>_
```

If the **malloc()** function cannot reserve the space requested the function returns a NULL value. This should be tested for when using **malloc()** to allow for that eventuality.

In the following example, the **malloc()** function reserves memory space for a user-specified quantity of integers. As the number of bytes used to store integers vary from system to system the **sizeof()** operator is used to calculate the total number of bytes to reserve.

mallocint.c

*This example does not need a cast because the pointer whose size is being set is an **int** data type.*

```c
#include <stdio.h>
#include <stdlib.h>

int main()
{
    int qty, *numbers, i;

    printf("How many integers would you like to store? ");
    scanf("%d", &qty );

    numbers = malloc( qty * sizeof(int) );
    if( numbers != NULL )
    {
        for(i=0; i<qty ; i++) numbers[i] = i+1;
        for(i=0; i<qty ; i++) printf("%d ", numbers[i]);
        printf("\n");
        free(numbers);              /* free allocated memory */
        return 0;
    }
    else{ printf("!!! Insufficient memory\n"); return 1; }
}
```

```
MyPrograms                                           _ □ ✕
C:\MyPrograms>gcc mallocint.c -o mallocint.exe

C:\MyPrograms>mallocint
How many integers would you like store? 20
1 2 3 4 5 6 7 8 9 10 11 12 13 14 15 16 17 18 19 20

C:\MyPrograms>mallocint
How many integers would you like store? 5000000000
!!! Insufficient memory

C:\MyPrograms>_
```

More memory management

There is another function in the **stdlib.h** header file that is very similar to the **malloc()** function described on the previous page. This one is named **calloc()** and has just two differences to the **malloc()** function.

Firstly, rather than the single argument required by **malloc()**, the **calloc()** function takes two integer arguments. These are multiplied together to specify how much memory space to allocate. Secondly, it clears all the allocated memory space to zero whereas **malloc()** leaves whatever values may already be there.

The differences can be clearly seen in this example:

calloc.c

*The **calloc()** function returns NULL if the request to allocate memory fails – just like the **malloc()** function does. This should normally be tested to allow for that eventuality, as in the previous example.*

```c
#include <stdio.h>
#include <stdlib.h>
int main()
{
  int *ptr1, *ptr2, i;
  ptr1 = calloc(10, sizeof(int));
  ptr2 = malloc(10);
  for(i=0; i<10; i++)
  {
    printf("calloc no.%d: %d\t", i, ptr1[i]);
    printf("malloc no.%d: %d\n", i, ptr2[i]);
  }
  return 0;
}
```

```
MyPrograms                                           _ □ ✕
C:\MyPrograms>gcc calloc.c -o calloc.exe

C:\MyPrograms>calloc
calloc no.0: 0    malloc no.0: 3998800
calloc no.1: 0    malloc no.1: 3998800
calloc no.2: 0    malloc no.2: 0
calloc no.3: 0    malloc no.3: 0
calloc no.4: 0    malloc no.4: 197121
calloc no.5: 0    malloc no.5: 524544
calloc no.6: 0    malloc no.6: 1819042147
calloc no.7: 0    malloc no.7: 1847616367
calloc no.8: 0    malloc no.8: 976760431
calloc no.9: 0    malloc no.9: 906571808

C:\MyPrograms>_
```

Memory that has been originally allocated a certain space with **malloc()** or **calloc()** can be increased with the **realloc()** function.

The example below uses the **realloc()** function to extend the memory allocated from its initial block of 5 to a larger block of 8:

realloc.c

```c
#include <stdio.h>
#include <stdlib.h>
int main()
{
 int i, *arr;

 arr = calloc(5, sizeof(int));
 if(arr!=NULL )
 {
  printf("Enter 5 integers, separated by a space:");
  for(i=0; i<5; i++) scanf("%d", &arr[i]);
  printf("Adding more space...\n");
  arr = realloc(8, sizeof(int));
  printf("Enter 3 more integers separated by a space:");
  for(i=5; i<8; i++) scanf("%d", &arr[i]);
  printf("Thanks.\nYour 8 entries were: ");
  for(i=0; i<8; i++) printf("%d, ", arr[i]);
  printf("\n");
  free(arr);
  return 0;
 }
 else {printf("!!! Insufficient Memory\n"); return 1;}
}
```

Like **calloc()**, the **realloc()** function *takes two arguments to specify the size of the memory space – and it returns a pointer when successful or a NULL value if it fails.*

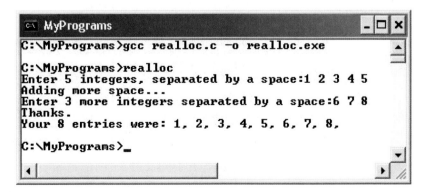

```
C:\MyPrograms>gcc realloc.c -o realloc.exe

C:\MyPrograms>realloc
Enter 5 integers, separated by a space:1 2 3 4 5
Adding more space...
Enter 3 more integers separated by a space:6 7 8
Thanks.
Your 8 entries were: 1, 2, 3, 4, 5, 6, 7, 8,

C:\MyPrograms>_
```

What next ?

This book will, hopefully, have given you a good understanding of the C programming language to the ANSI C standard. Like any language, be it a spoken language or a programming language, the best way to become proficient is to practice using it.

The Appendix to this book contains details of every function contained in the ANSI C library header files. It would be useful to experiment with each one so as to understand them better.

Creating C programs with a graphical user interface (GUI), such as applications for Windows, adds a lot of files to a program and these are best managed as a "Project" by a dedicated Integrated Development Environment (IDE).

Because the C++ language is an extension of the C language any IDE for C++ is also suitable for working with C programming. This does not necessarily mean that you have to know anything about the C++ programming language – you can simply use any C++ IDE to create C programs without regard to C++.

The Borland C++ Builder IDE (see www.borland.com) is favored by many C programmers, but it has extensions to the ANSI C standard that may result in less portable C program code.

www.microsoft.com

Another great alternative is Microsoft's Visual C++ IDE. This has latterly been incorporated into the Microsoft Visual Studio .net package, which requires an NT, Windows 2000 or XP platform – so Windows 95, 98 and ME users cannot enjoy its benefits.

The full-blown version of Visual Studio .net includes many different development tools, for C++, Visual Basic, and the latest language of C# (pronounced "see-sharp"). Earlier versions of the Microsoft Visual C++ 6 IDE can still be found for Windows 9.x. This is a great C/C++ development tool – at a lower cost too!

There is also a GUI front-end, for the GNU compiler used in this book, available free from Bloodshed Developments – for download at www.bloodshed.net. This free IDE is highly acclaimed – it's available for both Windows and Linux users, and you can't argue about the price.

You may, however, choose none of these options, and still enjoy a great future with C – it's around to stay. Happy C programming!

Reference section

This section of the book lists the standard ASCII key codes and every function contained in the standard C library, grouped by their header file. It includes descriptions of all the standard constants that specify minimum or maximum values, and those which define fixed floating-point numeric values.

Covers

Appendix

ASCII character codes

ASCII (American Standard Code for Information Interchange) is the standard representation of characters by numerical code. The non-printing character codes, originally developed for teletypes, are now rarely used for their intended original purpose.

There are also extended ASCII code sets from 128-255 (not listed) containing accented characters and symbols, but these sets do vary.

Note that the character represented by the character code 32 is not missing – it is, in fact, the non-printing space character. Also the character represented by character code 127 is the delete character.

Code	Char	Description
0	NUL	null
1	SOH	start of heading
2	STX	start of text
3	ETX	end of text
4	EOT	end of transmission
5	ENQ	enquiry
6	ACK	acknowledgement
7	BEL	bell
8	BS	backspace
9	TAB	horizontal tab
10	NL	newline
11	VT	vertical tab
12	FF	form feed
13	CR	carriage return
14	SO	shift out
15	SI	shift in

Code	Char	Description
16	DLE	data link escape
17	DC1	device control 1
18	DC2	device control 2
19	DC3	device control 3
20	DC4	device control 4
21	NAK	neg. acknowledge
22	SYN	synchronous file
23	ETB	end of trans. block
24	CAN	cancel
25	EM	end of medium
26	SUB	substitute
27	ESC	escape
28	FS	file separator
29	GS	group separator
30	RS	record separator
31	US	unit separator

To find out more about extended ASCII sets try the website at **www.asciitable.com** or search for ASCII on the web.

The term "ASCII" file just means a plain text file, such as those produced by Window's Notepad application.

Code	Char	Code	Char	Code	Char	Code	Char
32		56	8	80	P	104	h
33	!	57	9	81	Q	105	i
34	"	58	:	82	R	106	j
35	#	59	;	83	S	107	k
36	$	60	<	84	T	108	l
37	%	61	=	85	U	109	m
38	&	62	>	86	V	110	n
39	'	63	?	87	W	111	o
40	(	64	@	88	X	112	p
41	)	65	A	89	Y	113	q
42	*	66	B	90	Z	114	r
43	+	67	C	91	[	115	s
44	,	68	D	92	\	116	t
45	-	69	E	93	]	117	u
46	.	70	F	94	^	118	v
47	/	71	G	95	_	119	w
48	0	72	H	96	`	120	x
49	1	73	I	97	a	121	y
50	2	74	J	98	b	122	z
51	3	75	K	99	c	123	{
52	4	76	L	100	d	124		
53	5	77	M	101	e	125	}
54	6	78	N	102	f	126	~
55	7	79	O	103	g	127	del

Input/output functions

The functions and types defined in the **stdio.h** header represent almost one third of the C language library. It is used to introduce data into a program and generate output from a program.

A "stream" is a data source terminated by a "\n" newline character. It may be read or written by "opening" the stream, and terminated by "closing" it. Opening a stream returns a **FILE** type pointer in which information needed to control the stream is stored.

The functions listed in the following table perform file operations:

File-handling functions

FILE *fopen(const char *_filename_, const char _mode_) The **fopen()** function returns a **FILE** pointer, or **NULL** if the file cannot be opened. Any of the following modes may be specified in the function call: **r** open a text file for reading only **w** create a text file to write to – and discard any previous contents **a** append – open or create a text file for writing at the end of the file **r+** open a text file to update (read and write) **w+** open a text file to update (read and write discarding any previous contents) **a+** append – open or create a text file for update, for writing at the end of the file If the file being opened is a binary file a **b** should be added after the file mode, for instance **wb+**
FILE reopen(const char *_filename_ const char _mode_   **FILE *_stream_)** The **freopen()** function opens a file with the specified mode and associates the stream with it. It returns the stream or **NULL** if an error occurs. This function is normally used to change the files associated with **stdin**, **stdout** or **stderr**.
int fflush(FILE * _stream_) On an output stream this function causes any buffered data to be written immediately. It returns the **EOF** constant for a write error, or zero otherwise. A call to **fflush(NULL)** flushes all output streams.

int fclose(FILE *stream***)**
A call to **fclose()** flushes any unwritten data from the stream then closes the stream. It returns the **EOF** constant if an error occurs, or zero otherwise.

int remove(const char *filename***)**
This function removes the specified file – so that any subsequent attempt to open that file will fail. It returns a non-zero value if it cannot remove the file.

int rename(const char *old-name***, const char** *new-name***)**
The **rename()** function changes the name of the specified file, or it returns a non-zero value if it cannot rename the file.

FILE *tmpfile(void)
Calling **tmpfile()** creates a temporary file, with the file mode of **wb+,** that is removed when the program ends. This function returns a stream, or **NULL** if the file cannot be created

char *tmpnam(char *arr* [*L_tmpnam*] **)**
This function stores a string in an array and returns a unique valid file name pointer to that array. The *arr* array must have at least *L_tmpnam* characters. The **tmpnam()** function generates a diffrent name each time it is called.

int setvbuf(FILE *stream***, char** *buffer***, int** *mode,*
  size_t *size***)**
A call to **setvbuf()** sets buffering for the specified stream. It should be called after a stream has been opened but before any operation has been performed on it. Valid modes are **_IOFBF** to cause full buffering, **_IOLBF** for line buffering and **_IONBF** for no buffering. The *size* sets the buffer size. This function returns a non-zero value if an error occurs.

void setbuf(FILE *stream***, char** *buffer***)**
The **setbuf()** function defines how a stream should be buffered. It should be called after a stream has been opened but before any operation has been performed on it. The argument *buffer* points to an array to be used as the buffer.

Functions that format output

int fprintf(FILE *stream, const char *format, ...)
The **fprintf()** function converts and writes output to a specified file stream under the control of a format specifier. It returns the number of characters written, or a negative value if an error occurs.

int printf(const char *format, ...)
The **printf()** function writes and converts output to **stdout**. It is equivalent to **fprintf(stdout, const char *format, ...)**

int sprintf(char *s, const char *format, ...)
The **sprintf()** function is the same as **printf()** except the output is written into the specified string, and terminated with a **\0** null character

vprintf(const char *format, va_list arg)
vfprintf(FILE *stream, const char *format, va_list arg)
vsprintf(char *s, const char *format, va_list arg)
These three functions are equivalent to the corresponding **printf()** functions except that their variable argument list is replaced by an argument of the **va_list** type. Refer to the **stdarg.h** header file functions on page 180 for more details.

Functions that format input

int fscanf(FILE *stream, const char *format, ...)
The **fscanf()** function reads from a specified stream under the control of a format specifier and assigns converted values to subsequent arguments. It returns the number of input items converted or the EOF constant if the end of the file is met, or if an error occurs

int scanf(constant char *format, ...)
The **scanf()** function reads and converts input to stdin. It is equivalent to **fscanf(stdin, const char *format, ...)**

int sscanf(char *s, const char *format, ...)
The **sscanf()** function is the same as **scanf()** except the input is read from the specified string

Format specifiers for output

In C a "%" prefix denotes a format specifier. All **printf()** format specifiers are listed below, and those for **scanf()** on the next page.

Character	printf() converts to
d, i	**int** data type, signed decimal
o	**int** data type, unsigned octal without a leading zero
x, X	**int** unsigned hexadecimal. 0x uses lowercase, such as 0xff, and 0X uses uppercase, such as 0XFF
u	**int** data type, unsigned decimal
c	**int** single character, after conversion to **char** data type
s	**char** pointer to a string, ending with the \0 null character
f	**double** data type in the form xxx.yyyyyy where the number of digits after the decimal point is set by precision. The default precision is 6 digits.
e, E	**double** data type in the form xx.yyyyyye±zz or xx.yyyyyyE±zz where the number of digits after the decimal point is set by precision. The default precision is 6 digits.
g, G	**double** data type printed as %e or %E conversioniif the exponent is less than -, otherwise printed as a %f conversion
p	the memory address of a pointer
n	not a conversion, but stores the number of characters written so far by the call to the **printf()** function in an **int** pointer argument
%	not a conversion, prints a '%'

Format specifiers for input

Character	scanf() converts to
d	**int** data type, signed decimal integer
i	**int** data type which may be in octal (leading 0) or hexadecimal (leading 0x or 0X)
o	**int** data type, octal integer with or without a leading zero
u	**int** data type, unsigned decimal
x	**int** hexadecimal integer, with or without leading 0x or 0X
c	**char** characters, into a specified array. Reads the number of characters stated in its width field (default is 1) without adding a final **\0** null character. Stops reading when a space is met
s	a string of non-whitespace **char** characters, into an array. The array must be big enough for all the characters plus a final **\0** null character
e, f, g	**float** data type, optionally beginning with a sign, then followed by a string of numbers. These may contain a decimal point, and an optional exponent field containing an "E" or "e" followed by a possibly signed integer
p	a memory address, in the same form as that output by the **%p** conversion with **printf()**
n	not a conversion, but stores the number of characters read so far by the call to the **scanf()** function in an **int** pointer argument
[...]	matches a string specified in the square brackets to those in the input stream and adds a **\0** null character
[^...]	matches all ASCII characters in the input stream <u>except</u> those specified in the square brackets, and adds a **\0** null character

Functions for character input and output

---

int fgetc(FILE **stream***)**
returns the next character of the specified stream as a **char**, or the **EOF** constant if at the end of the file or an error occurs

---

char *fgets(char **s***, int** *n***, FILE ****stream***)**
reads the next *n-1* characters into the specified stream then adds a **\0** null character at the end of the array. This function returns *s* or NULL if at the end of the file or if an error occurs

---

int fputc(int *c***, FILE ****stream***)**
writes the character *c* to the specified stream and returns the character written or **EOF** if an error occurs

---

int fputs(const char **s***, FILE ****stream***)**
writes the string *s* to the specified stream and returns non-negative, of **EOF** if an error occurs

---

int getc(FILE **stream***)**
the **getc()** function is the macro equivalent of **fgetc()**

---

int getchar(void)
the **getchar()** function is equivalent to **getc(stdin)**

---

char *gets(char **s***)**
reads the next input line into an array, replacing its final newline character with a **\0** null character. It returns *s* or NULL if at the end of the file, or if an error occurs

---

int putc(int *c***, FILE ****stream***)**
the **putc()** function is the macro equivalent of **fputc()**

---

int putchar(int *c* **)** is equivalent to **putc(***c***, stdout)**

---

int puts(const char *s **)**
writes the string *s* and a newline character to **stdout**. It returns non-negative or **EOF** if an error occurs

---

int ungetc(int *c***, FILE ****stream***)**
pushes the character *c* back onto the specified stream where it is returned on the next read. Only one pushback character per stream is guaranteed and **EOF** cannot be pushed back. **ungetc()** returns the character pushed back, or **EOF** on error

Functions for direct stream input and output

The **fread()** and **fwrite()** functions contained in the **stdio.h** header file are most effect to read and write entire text files:

---

size_t fread(void *ptr*, **size_t** *size*,
                               size_t *nobj*, **FILE** **stream*)
the **fread()** function reads from the specified stream into the specified *ptr* array pointer at most *nobj* objects of *size* size.
fread() returns the number of objects it has read, which may be less than the number requested in the function call.
The status of **fread()** can be tested as it proceeds using the **feof()** and **ferror()** functions – see the error functions listed on the opposite page

---

size_t fwrite(const void **ptr*, **size_t** *size*,
                               size_t*nobj*, **FILE** **stream*)
the **fwrite()** function writes from the specified *ptr* pointer *nobj* objects of *size* size. It returns the number of objects that it has written. If an error occurs the returned value will be less than that requested by *nobj* in the function call.

Error functions

Many of the standard functions in the C library set status indicators when an error occurs, or when the end of a file is reached. These indicators can be tested using the error functions listed in the table below. Also the integer expression **errno**, defined in the **errno.h** header file, may contain an error code giving more information about the most recent error.

---

void clearerr(FILE **stream***)**
the **clearerr()** function clears the end of file and error indicators for the specified stream

---

int feof(FILE **stream***)**
the **feof()** function returns a non-zero vale if the end of file indicator is set for the specified stream

---

int ferror(FILE **stream***)**
the **ferror()** function returns a non-zero value if the error indicator is set for the specified stream

---

void perror(const char **s***)**
the **perror()** function prints an implementation defined error message associated with the integer value contained in the **errno** expression. See also the **strerror()** function in the **string.h** header file on page 175.

File-positioning functions

A file stream is processed by moving through the characters it contains one by one. The functions in the following table can be used to manipulate the position in a file stream:

---

int fseek(FILE *_stream,_ long _offset,_ int _original_)
the **fseek()** function sets the file position in the specified stream. Subsequent reading, or writing, begins at the new position. The new position is determined by specifying how far to _offset_ the position from its _original_ position. Optionally the third argument of the **fseek()** function can be specified as **SEEK_SET** (beginning), **SEEK_CUR** (current position) or **SEEK_END** (end of file). For a text stream the _offset_ must be either zero or a value returned by the **ftell()** function with the original position specified as **SEEK_SET**. The **fseek()** function returns non-zero if an error occurs.

---

long ftell(FILE *_stream_)
the **ftell()** function returns the current file position of the specified stream, or -1L if an error occurs

---

int fgetpos(FILE *_stream_, fpos_t *_ptr_)
the **fgetpos()** records the current file position of the specified stream in the specified _ptr_ pointer as a special **fpos_t** type. This function returns a non-zero value if an error occurs.

---

int fsetpos(FILE *_stream_, const fpos_t *_ptr_)
the **fsetpos()** function positions the file pointer in the specified stream at the position recorded by **fgetpos()** in the _ptr_ pointer. **fsetpos()** returns a non-zero value on error

---

Character test functions

The **ctype.h** header file contains functions for testing characters. In each case, the character must be specified as the function's argument. The functions return a non-zero value (true) when the tested condition is met, or zero if it is not. Additionally, this header file contains two functions for converting the case of letters. All of the functions in the **ctype.h** header file are listed in the table below together with a description:

Function	Description
isalpha(*c* **)**	is the character a letter?
isalnum(*c* **)**	is the character a letter or a number?
iscntrl(*c* **)**	is the character a control character?
isdigit(*c* **)**	is the character a decimal digit?
isgraph(*c* **)**	is the character any printing character except a space?
islower(*c* **)**	is the character a lowercase letter?
isprint(*c* **)**	is the character any printing character including a space?
ispunct(*c* **)**	is the character any printing character except a space, a letter, or a digit?
isspace(*c* **)**	is the character a space, formfeed, newline, carriage return, horizontal tab, or vertical tab?
isupper(*c* **)**	is the character an uppercase letter?
isxdigit(*c* **)**	is the character a hexadecimal digit?
int tolower(int *c* **)**	convert the character to lowercase
int toupper(int *c* **)**	convert the character to uppercase

String functions

The **string.h** header file contains the following functions that can be used to compare and manipulate text strings:

Function	Description
char *strcpy(s1, s2)	copy s2 to s1, then return s1
char *strncpy(s1, s2, n)	copy n characters of s2 to s1, then return s1
char *strcat(s1, s2)	concatenate s2 to the end of s1, then return s1
char *strncat(s1, s2, n)	concatenate n characters of s2 to the end of s1, then return s1
int strcmp(s1, s2)	compare s1 to s2, then return < 0 if s1 < s2, 0 if s1== s2, or > 0 if s1 > s2
int strncmp(s1, s2, n)	compare n characters of s1 to s2, then return < 0 if s1 < s2, 0 if s1 == s2, or > 0 if s1 > s2
char *strchr(s, c)	return a pointer to the first occurrence of c in s, or NULL if not present
char *strrchr(s, c)	return a pointer to the last occurrence of c in s, or NULL if not present
size_t strspn(s1, s2)	return length of prefix of s1 consisting of characters in s2
size_t strcspn(s1, s2)	return length of prefix of s1 consisting of characters <u>not</u> in s2

Function	Description
char *strpbrk(*s1, s2***)**	return a pointer to the first occurrence in *s1* of any character of *s2*, or NULL if none are present
char *strstr(*s1, s2***)**	return a pointer to the first occurrence of *s2* in *s1* or NULL if not present
size_t strlen(*s***)**	return the length of *s*
char *strerror(*n***)**	return a pointer to the implementation-defined string associated with the error code*n*
char *strtok(*s1, s2***)**	search *s1* for tokens delimited by characters from *s2*
void *memcpy(*s1, s2, n***)**	copy *n* characters from *s2* to *s1*, then return *s1*
void *memmove(*s1, s2, n***)**	same as **memcpy()** but it works even when the objects overlap
int memcmp(*s1, s2, n***)**	compare the first *n* characters of *s1* with *s2*, return as with the **strcmp()** function
void *memchr(*s, c, n***)**	return a pointer to the first occurrence of character *c* in *s*, or return NULL if not present in the first *n* characters
void *memset(*s, c, n***)**	place character *c* into the first *n* characters of *s*, then return *s*

Math functions

The **math.h** header file contains functions that perform mathematical calculations. All the functions are listed in the table below together with a description of the calculation they perform. In the table, *x* and *y* are **double** data types and *n* is a **int** data type. All the functions return the result of their calculation as a **double** data type:

Function	Description
sin(*x*)	return the sine of *x*
cos(*x*)	return the cosine of *x*
tan(*x*)	return the tangent of *x*
asin(*x*)	return the arcsine of *x*
acos(*x*)	return the arccosine of *x*
atan(*x*)	return the arctangent of *x*
atan2(*y*, *x*)	return the angle (in radians) from the *x* axis to a point *y*
sinh(*x*)	return the hyperbolic sine of *x*
cosh(*x*)	return the hyperbolic cosine of *x*
tanh(*x*)	return the hyperbolic tangent of *x*
exp(*x*)	return **e** (the base of natural logarithms) raised to the power *x*
log(*x*)	return the natural logarithm of *x*
log10(*x*)	return the base10 logarithm of *x*
pow(*x*, *y*)	return *x* raised to the power *y*
sqrt(*x*)	return the square root of *x*

Function	Description
ceil(x**)**	return the smallest integer not less than x, as a double
floor(x**)**	return the largest integer not greater than x, as a double
fabs(x**)**	return the absolute value of x
ldexp(x, n**)**	return x multiplied by 2 and raised to the power n
frexp(x, **int** *exp**)**	decompose x into two parts – return a mantissa between 0.5 and 1, and store exponent in exp
modf(x, **double** *ip**)**	split x into integer and fraction – return the fractional part, and store the integral part in ip
fmod(x, y**)**	return the remainder of dividing x by y

Utility functions

double atof(const char **s***)** converts *s* to a **double**
int atoi(const char **s***)** converts *s* to an **int**
long atol(const char **s***)** converts *s* to a **long**
double strtod(const char **s***, char** ***endp***)** converts the initial part of *s* to a **double**, ignoring leading whitespace. A pointer to the rest of *s* is stored in **endp*.
long strtol(const char **s***, char** ***endp***, int** *b***)** converts the initial part of *s* to a long using base *b*. A pointer to the rest of *s* is stored in **endp*.
unsigned long strtoul(const char **s***, char** ***endp***, int** *b***)** the **strtoul()** function is the same as the **strtol()** function except that the returned result is an **unsigned long**
int rand(void) returns a psuedo-random number between zero and an implementation-dependent maximum of at least 32,767
void srand(unsigned int *seed***)** sets the seed for a new sequence of random numberssupplied by **rand()**. The initial seed is 1.
void *calloc(size_t *nobj***, size_t** *size***)** returns a pointer to memory space for an array of *nobj* objects of size*size*, or NULL if the request cannot be met. This space is initialized to zero bytes.
void *malloc(size_t *size***)** returns a pointer to memory space for an object of size*size*, or NULL if the request fails. This space is uninitialized.
void *realloc(void **p***, size_t** *size***)** changes the size of an object pointed to by*p* to *size*. **realloc()** returns a pointer to the new space or NULL if the request fails
void free(void **p***)** the **free()** function deallocates the memory space pointed to by *p*. Note that *p* must be a pointer to memory space previously allocated by **calloc()**, **malloc()** or **realloc()**.

void abort(void) causes the program to end abnormally

void exit(int *status***)**
causes the program to end normally. The value of *status* is returned to the system. Optionally **EXIT_SUCCESS** and **EXIT_FAILURE** can be used to specify the *status* values

int atexit(void (**fcn***)(void))**
registers the function *fcn* to be called when the program terminates. **atexit()** returns a non-zero value if unsuccessful

int system(const char **s***)**
passes the string s to the environment for processing. The return value is implementation-dependent

char *getenv(const char **name***)**
returns the environment string associated with *name*, or NULL if no string is associated with *name* in that environment. The details are implementation-dependent.

void *bsearch(const void **key***, const void ****base***,**
       size_t *n***, size_t** *size***,**
           int (*cmp)(const void **keyval***, const void ****datum***))**
searches *base*[0]...*base*[*n*-1] for an item that matches *key*. It returns a pointer to the matching item if successful, otherwise it returns a NULL value. Items in the array *base* must be in ascending order.

void qsort(void **base***, size_t** *n***, size_t** *size***,**
               int(*cmp)(const void *, const void *))
sorts into ascending order an array *base*[0]...*base*[*n*-1] of objects of size *size*. The comparison function **cmp()** is the same as that in the **bsearch()** function.

int abs(int *n***)** returns the absolute value of **int** *n*

long labs(long *n***)** returns the absolute value of **long** *n*

div_t ldiv(long *num***, long** *denom***)**
divides *num* by *denom* and stores the results in members of a structure of type **ldiv_t**. Its **quot** member stores the quotient result and its **rem** member stores the remainder result

Diagnostic functions

The **assert()** function, contained in the **assert.h** header file, can be used to add diagnostics to a program:

```
void assert(int expression);
```

If *expression* is zero when **assert(***expression***)** is executed, the function will print a message on **stderr**, such as:

```
Assertion failed: expression, file filename, line nnn
```

The **assert()** function then attempts to terminate the program.

Argument functions

The **stdarg.h** header file contains functions that can be used to step through a list of function arguments without first knowing their number and type. Due to the nature of these functions, they must be implemented as "macros", within the function's body.

The list of arguments is assigned to a special data type named **va_list**. The functions listed in the following table manipulate a variable named "args" of the **va_list** type:

va_start(va_list *args*, *lastarg*) must be called once to initialize the **va_list** named *args* at the position in the list of the last known argument *lastarg*
va_arg(va_list *args*, *data-type*) After the **va_list** *args* has been initialized with **va_start()** each successive call to **va_arg()** will return the value of the next argument in the *args* list as the specified data type.
va_end(va_list *args*) must be called once after the arguments in the **va_list** *args* have been processed, before the function is exited

Date & time functions

The **time.h** header file contains functions for manipulating date and time. Some of these functions process "Calendar time", which is based on the Gregorian calendar. This is stated in seconds elapsed since the Epoch (00:00:00 GMT January 1st, 1970).

Other functions contained in **time.h** process "Local time", which is the translation of Calendar time accounting for time zone.

The data type **time_t** is used to describe both Calendar time and Local time.

A struct named **tm** contains the components of Calendar time, which are listed in the following table:

Component	Description
int tm_sec	seconds after the minute, 0-61
int tm_min	minutes after the hour, 0-59
int_tm_hour	hours since midnight, 0-23
int tm_mday	day of the month, 1-31
int tm_mon	months since January, 0-11
int tm_year	years since 1900
int tm_wday	days since Sunday, 0-6
int tm_yday	days since January 1st, 0-365
int tm_isdst	Daylight Saving Time flag

The **tm_isdst** component is positive if Daylight Saving is in effect, zero if it is not, and negative if the information is unavailable.

The functions contained in the **time.h** header file are listed in the table on the next page.

The **time.h** header file contains the functions listed below that can be used to manipulate date and time:

clock_t clock(void) returns the processor time used by the program since it started, or -1 if unavailable
time_t time(time_t *tp*) returns the current calendar time, or -1 if unavailable
double difftime(time_t *time2*, **time_t** *time1*) returns *time2-time1*, expressed in seconds
time_t mktime(struct tm *tp*) converts the local time in the structure *tp into calendar time
char *asctime(const struct tm *tp*) converts the time in the struct *tp into a standard string
char *ctime(const time_t *tp*) converts calendar time to local time
struct tm *gmtime(const time_t *tp*) converts calendar time into Coordinated Universal Time (UTC or GMT)
struct tm *localtime(const time_t *tp*) converts the calendar time *tp into local time
size_t strftime(char *s*, **size_t** *smax*, **const char** *fmt*, **const struct tm** *tp*) formats the time *tp into a chosen format *fmt.

The **strftime()** function formats selected components of the **tm** struct according to the stated format specifier. All the possible format specifiers that can be used with **strftime()** are listed in the table on the opposite page.

Specifier	Description
%a	abbreviated weekday name
%A	full weekday name
%b	abbreviated month name
%B	full month name
%c	local date and time representation
%d	day of the month, 01 - 31
%H	hour (24-hour clock), 00 - 23
%I	hour (12-hour clock), 01-12
%j	day of the year, 001 - 366
%m	month of the year, 01 - 12
%M	minute, 00 - 59
%p	local equivalent of AM or PM
%S	second, 00 - 61 (to account for leap seconds)
%U	week number of the year (Sunday as the first day of the week), 00 - 53
%w	weekday number, 0 - 6 (Sunday is 0)
%W	week number of the year (Monday as the first day of the week), 00 - 53
%x	local date representation
%X	local time representation
%y	year without century, 00 - 99
%Y	year with century
%Z	time zone name, if available

Jump functions

The **setjmp.h** header is used for controlling low-level calls and provides a means to avoid the normal call and return sequence.

---

int setjmp(jmp_buf *env***)**
low-level function used in conditional tests to save the environment in the *env* variable, then return zero

---

void longjmp(jmp_buf *env***, int** *value***)**
restores an evironment that has been saved in the*env* variable by **setjmp()** – as if **setjmp()** had returned the *value*

Signal functions

The **signal.h** header contains functions for handling exceptional conditions that may arise during the execution of a program:

---

void (*signal (int *sig***, void (****handler***) (int))) (int)**|
the **signal()** function specifies how subsequent signals will be handled. The *handler* can be **SIG_DFL**, an implementation-defined default, or **SIG_IGN** to ignore the signal.
Valid *sig* signals include:
  SIGABRT : abnormal termination
  SIGFPE : arithmetic error
  SIGILL : illegal instruction
  SIGINT : external interruption
  SIGSEGV : access outside memory limit
  SIGTERM : termination request sent to the program
The function returns the previous value of *handler* for that specific signal, or **SIG_ERR** if an error occurs. When a *sig* signal next occurs the signal is restored to its default behaviour then the signal-handler is called. If this returns, execution resumes at the point where the signal occurred

---

int raise(int *sig***)**
attempts to send the signal *sig* to the program and returns a non-zero value if the attempt is unsuccessful

---

Limit constants

The table below lists constants related to maximum and minimum numerical limits. Their values vary according to implementation. Where a value is given, in brackets, it indicates a minimum size for that constant – but larger values may, in fact, be imposed.
Programs should not assume that any implementation-dependent constant will be of a particular value.

Constant	Value
CHAR_BIT	number of bits in a **char** (8)
CHAR_MAX	maximum value of **char** (UCHAR_MAX or SCHAR_MAX)
CHAR_MIN	minimum value of **char** (zero or SCHAR_MIN)
INT_MAX	maximum value of **int** (+32,787)
INT_MIN	miniumum value of **int** (-32,767)
LONG_MAX	maximum value of long (+2,147,483,647)
LONG_MIN	minimum value of long (-2,147,483,647)
SCHAR_MAX	maximum value of signed**char** (+127)
SCHAR_MIN	minimum value of signed**char** (-127)
SHRT_MAX	maximum value of short (+32,767)
SHRT_MIN	minimum value of short (-32,767)
UCHAR_MAX	maximum value of unsigned**char** (+255)
UINT_MAX	maximum value of unsigned**int** (+65,535)
ULONG_MAX	maximum value of unsigned long (+4,294,967,295)
USHRT_MAX	maximum value of unsigned short (+65,535)

Float constants

The table below lists constants related to floating-point arithmetic. Their values vary according to implementation. Where a value is given, in brackets, it indicates a minimum size for that constant.

Constant	Value
FLT_RADIX	radix of float exponent representations (2)
FLT_ROUNDS	rounding to the nearest number
FLT_DIG	number of precision digits (6)
FLT_EPSILON	smallest number **x**, where $1.0 + x \neq 1.0$ (1E-5)
FLT_MANT_DIG	number of FLT_RADIX mantissa digits
FLT_MAX	maximum floating point number (1E+37)
FLT_MAX_EXP	largest number **n**, where FLT_RADIX^n -1 is a valid number
FLT_MIN	minimum floating point number (1E-37)
FLT_MIN_EXP	smallest number **n** where 10^n is valid
DBL_DIG	number of double precision digits (10)
DBL_EPSILON	smallest number **x**, where $1.0 + x \neq 1.0$ (1E-9)
DBL_MANT_DIG	number of FLT_RADIX mantissa digits
DBL_MAX	maximum double float number (1E+37)
DBL_MAX_EXP	largest number **n**, where FLT_RADIX^n -1 is a valid number
DBL_MIN	minimum double float number (1E-37)
DBL_MIN_EXP	smallest number **n** where 10^n is valid

Index

G

H

I

L

M

N

O

P

Q

R

S